"THE REFRIGERATOR"

&

THE MONSTERS OF THE MIDWAY

WILLIAM PERRY & THE CHICAGO BEARS

By BRIAN HEWITT

AN ASSOCIATED FEATURES BOOK

A SIGNET BOOK

NEW AMERICAN LIBRARY

ACKNOWLEDGMENTS

The author and editor wish to acknowledge the many sources who helped make this book happen, including Bob Bradley and Tim Bourret of Clemson University, Ginny Southworth of the Aiken (S.C.) *Standard*, George Gardner of the Greenville (S.C.) *News*, Bill Tobin, Ken Valdiserri and Bryan Harlan of the Chicago Bears, Dick Maxwell of the NFL, Phyllis Hollander of Associated Features, Gerry Burstein of G&H/Soho, Ltd., Laurie Harris of JetSet, and the various contributing photographers.

Brian Hewitt and Zander Hollander

Designer: Gerry Burstein

Cover Design: George Cornell

PHOTO CREDITS

Front cover: Vernon Biever
Back cover: Bill Smith
AP/Wide World 7, 20, 31, 36, 41, 43, 45, 47, 53
Aiken *Standard* 8, 63
James Biever 44, 48
John Biever 25
Vernon Biever, 21, 23, 24, 33, 49, 51
ABC-TV 30
Chicago Bears 38, 39, 40
Clemson 12, 15, 17
Greenville *News* 11, 14
Vic Milton 4, 34
Bill Smith 3, 61
UPI 22, 26, 27, 28
Phil Velasquez, Chicago *Sun-Times* 56
The Jeff MacNelly cartoon on page 54 reprinted by permission of Tribune Media Services.

 SIGNET TRADEMARK REG. U.S. PAT. OFF. AND FOREIGN COUNTRIES
REGISTERED TRADEMARK—MARCA REGISTRADA
HECHO EN SECAUCUS, U.S.A.

SIGNET, SIGNET CLASSIC, MENTOR, PLUME, MERIDIAN, and NAL BOOKS
are published by New American Library, 1633 Broadway, New York 10019.

First Printing December 1985

1 2 3 4 5 6 7 8 9

PRINTED IN THE UNITED STATES OF AMERICA

CONTENTS

INTRODUCTION

It all happened so fast. Before anybody knew what to think and before anybody dreamed of the consequences, Bear head coach Mike Ditka had slipped a rookie defensive tackle into his offensive backfield. On national television.

Monday night, October 21, 1985, a nation turned its hungry eyes to William (The Refrigerator) Perry.

Perry responded by throwing the block heard round the football world. Said *Sports Illustrated*: "When the TV monitors showed the first slo-mo of Perry enveloping Green Bay linebacker George Cumby the way a corpuscle attacks a germ, shrieks of 'Mockery!' and 'Inertia!' rang out."

It got better.

The next time the Bears got the ball near the goal line, Ditka used the 308-pound Perry as a ballcarrier. Quicker than you can say "$E = MC^2$", Perry burst off right tackle for one yard and a touchdown. Suddenly reality was a Mack truck careening downhill without any brakes.

"This could be the start of someone big," said Los Angeles *Times* columnist Mike Downey.

"The best use of fat since the invention of bacon," wrote columnist Ray Sons in the Chicago *Sun-Times*.

The Bears beat the Packers, 23-7, that night as Perry threw another crushing block on Cumby to pave the way for a Walter Payton touchdown. Two weeks later he caught a touchdown pass. Then he appeared on "Late Night with David Letterman." Johnny Carson was next in line. Fan clubs sprouted up across the country like atomic mushrooms.

The Bears, meanwhile, won their first 11 games and hurtled toward Super Bowl XX. Their success served to legitimize the growing national focus on Perry. So the balladeers worked overtime. Joke writers feasted. The good-natured Perry laughed louder than anybody—and all the way to the bank.

"Everybody has something to say smart," Perry said. "But as long as nobody comes up and slaps me in the face, I don't feel no real grief. I've always thought that if you're different, it's up to you to make friends with the other guy. My sense of humor can carry me. I laugh along. I figure that God shapes everybody to a purpose."

Perry's shape was his purpose. And the public sensed their gentle giant was comfortable with that. They loved the guy. Soon "The Refrigerator" was simply "Fridge." By midseason the normal $300 appearance fee paid to Bear rookies had skyrocketed to $5,000 for Perry.

The Refrigerator nickname had stemmed from a publicity poster distributed in college by the Clemson sports information department. The poster is now a collector's item. Meanwhile, a singer who called himself "Bongo Billiards" waxed lyrical in a song entitled, "They Call in The Fridge."

A sample verse: "I go both ways/ But don't get me wrong/ On offense and defense, I'm equally strong/ I eat linemen for lunch/ I eat quarterbacks for dinner/ To wash it all down, I drink paint thinner."

William Perry didn't really drink paint thinner. But growing up in rural Aiken, South Carolina, he had eaten everything his mother had ever put in front of him. Now it was time to weigh the outcome.

5

CHAPTER ONE

GROWING UP

When William Perry was eight months old his mother's stepfather leaned down and peered into his eyes. Inez Perry still remembers: "He looked at William and said, 'He's going to be something special, you watch what I tell you. I don't know what it is, but there's something about those funny eyes.'"

"I just wish," added Inez Perry after her 10th child had become a national celebrity, "he were here today to see."

William Perry was always large—he weighed 13½ pounds at birth, on December 16, 1962. "I was big even when I was little," he would later say.

Inez and Hollie Perry eventually produced a total of 12 children—eight boys and four girls—in the rural community of Aiken, South Carolina. Hollie, the father, is only 5-11½, 200 pounds. Inez is a sturdy-legged 5-9½. "The size of the children comes from my wife," said Hollie.

Aiken is comprised mostly of simple frame houses. But its outskirts are dotted with horse farms owned by wealthy men. Just a hoot and a holler down the road and across the state line is Augusta, Georgia, site of the famed Masters golf tournament. The Perry family wasn't poor. But money was always scarce.

"My daddy worked. My mom worked. And I worked on Saturdays," said Perry. "I raked yards and cut grass and hedges. I had to do something. Mom and Dad couldn't give me no allowance. So I had to find something that would give me some money.

"I was always out there making money or doing something. That's where I got my extra money before I went to college." Perry often shared his raking gigs with younger brother Michael Dean. They would pool their profits to buy cookies and cakes. "We'd buy about 100 cookies and he would give me five," said Michael Dean.

Inez and Hollie raised their children at 39 Kershaw St. in a modest three-bedroom house across the street from a recreation center. It was also just a block from the local jail. But it was a million miles from trouble. "They were all nice kids," said South Aiken football coach Gary Smallen of the Perry brood. "And very well respected." Smallen would inherit Perry's two younger brothers, Darrell and Michael Dean, after the school district split.

Inez and Hollie had spent the first 11 years of their marriage in a housing project before the money Hollie saved from his work as a painter enabled them to move into the house. Meanwhile Inez had learned two things from working as a cook at nearby Aiken Prep: how to prepare a meal and the importance of good attendance. When he graduated from Aiken High, William received a pen for never having missed a day of school. "It didn't matter if I was sick," he said. "I still put my pants on regardless." That record extended to the football field. To this day Perry has never missed a game due to injury.

"The No. 1 thing is I wanted them to get their high school diplomas,"

Inez and Hollie Perry raised 12 children, the 10th of whom was a 13½-pounder named William.

said Inez. "And all of them did. And practically all of them have been in college. You don't see that happen much with 12 kids."

And of course there was always perfect attendance at mealtime. "I never put a limit on what they could eat," said Inez. "I don't care what it was. Up to today, I don't try to tell them not to eat something. And it seems all of them are big eaters, even the girls."

But soon the boys grew out of sight. "I used to tackle them," said Shirley, the oldest daughter. "But after a while they told me to sit down. They just kept getting bigger and bigger. It amazed me."

William got the biggest. "You can tell William always got to the table first," was the way Michael Dean put it.

But even Leonard, the smallest brother, turned out to be 6 feet, 200 pounds. Freddie filled out to 320 pounds. Michael Dean reached 275 at one point. Hollie Jr. topped out at 250. And others ranged in the 230s.

When New York *Daily News* columnist Jimmy Breslin phoned the Perrys, Inez described the typical evening menu:

Four chickens. ("They're wild over fried chicken.")

Special hamburger dish: Seven pounds of ground beef. Add tomato paste, tomato sauce, A-1 sauce, special back-of-town South Carolina hot sauce, quart and a half of water. Add 4½ pounds of macaroni and American cheese to suit.

Two pans of corn bread. ("The kind of pans they use in bakeries. Big things you need both hands and a knee under to hold.")

One pot (great big pot) of collard greens.

Bread. Two loaves. (Kingsize.)

Pound and a half of butter.

Whole lot of iced tea.

Milk. One gallon.

"If something wasn't ready," Inez told Breslin, "William didn't say

7

Football wasn't William's only sport. He was a force in basketball as well at Aiken High.

The Aiken High Booster Club and the American Legion bought jackets for the 1978 Region 3-AAA football champions. Coach Eddie Buck helps William don his jacket. Teammate Andy Ratchford is on the left.

anything. He would just take himself into the kitchen and stir himself up something. He would make a cake."

In between meals and organized sports at school, the Perry brothers became an institution in neighborhood games. Typically it was the Perry brothers against everybody else. "We'd beat them in football and then beat them in basketball," said William. "We only lost when we got tired."

"Everyone seemed to love them and want to be with them," said Inez.

William still heads right for the basketball court when he gets back to Aiken. "Me and all my brothers go to the gym and play all the time. I like to shoot it. And once I get hot, it's over."

Freddie, in his 30s now, still plays semipro football for the Augusta Eagles. Darrell, at 210, is a starting defensive back for Gardner-Webb. Hollie Jr., Willie and Robert were two-sport athletes at Tuskegee.

But William and Michael Dean have taken their talents the farthest.

8

Clemson defensive coordinator Tom Harper predicted Michael Dean, like his brother, would become one of the best defensive linemen in Clemson history. This year he dieted down to 255 but suffered a severe ankle sprain in August and never completely recovered.

Where William was gentle, Michael Dean was rough. "Michael Dean has to be the most destructive person I know," said coach Smallen. "He's a bull in a china cabinet. He'll destroy the 45-pound weights in the weight room, and he's destructive on linemen.

Older brother William weighed 240 pounds by the time he reached ninth grade. Inez never worried about him, but constantly feared for the other kids. "I was afraid William would hurt somebody," she said. "When he was in the eighth grade he was playing with kids between the ninth and 12th grade. William just grew and grew. When he was around 10 or 12, he looked like he was a person 16 or 17 years old."

To be sure, William wasn't perfect. But, said Inez, "I wouldn't stand a bad child."

"I wanted everyone to like them and for them to be nice people," she told Chris Smith of the Greenville (S.C.) *News*. "So I knew I had to do my part." The hardest part was keeping the furniture intact. "The most problem I had was with them flopping in chairs," said Inez. "We'd be replacing chairs all the time. And I told them if they wanted to 'rassle' they had to hit the door. They knew I didn't like fighting or people to mistreat each other. If they passed the first angry word, I would pass the second and third."

"She kept us in line," said Perry. "It just took a couple of licks and we knew mother would use the straps." The last lick Perry ever got from his mother was in the seventh grade. He already weighed 220 pounds. "I was kind of bad," he said. "But she straightened me out with just one lick.

"I had hit a little boy and when she came out on the porch I thought she was going to call me inside. But she hit me across the street with a flyswatter. After that, I figured I'd better do my hitting on the football field."

A school principal named T.W. Williams had introduced William to PeeWee football in East Aiken. "We had no money for me to play," said William. "So Mr. Williams let me cut the grass at the school, and he paid for my PeeWee football. That's how I got my start."

"When he was in the eighth grade he weighed 235 or 240," said Aiken High coach Eddie Buck. "And he looked like a 17-year-old who had been on a good weight program."

"Undoubtedly there must be something in the Perry genes," Clemson's Harper would say later.

"But we really didn't do William justice in high school because we couldn't spend the time with him in drills," said Buck. "He just couldn't practice. I really think he made more kids quit the team than come out. In one-on-one drills, a lot of times guys would quit instead of going against him. I don't think William ever reached his potential, because he was never truly challenged."

Except by his own rapid growth. "We were getting ready to have the pictures taken for the yearbook his senior year," recalled Buck. "And William couldn't get his old pants on. His thighs had grown from about 31 inches the year before to 32½. So the seamstress had to cut apart another pair of game pants and sew the two pants together. I still have those as a souvenir."

At home William was too heavy for the top bunk. But sleeping problems caused him to kick the top bunk when he slept on the bottom. It was a no-win situation. "The top bunk went to the ceiling when he kicked it," said Inez. "I remember one of my sons, who was in the bunk, telling me, 'I was floating on air.'"

During the summer between ninth and 10th grade Perry met Aiken's Sherry Broadwater, the pretty girl he would marry after his freshman year at Clemson. Soon they started dating. "At the end of the 10th grade we started getting serious," said William. "We've been together ever since."

The first time William asked Sherry to dance, she told him to go away. She thought he was too big. In time, she changed her mind. "I stopped thinking of William as big," she said. "I just started thinking of him as muscle-built. If William was to see someone as big as he was with a lot of fat, not muscle, he would laugh and say, 'I wouldn't let myself get that big.'"

Perry still remembers the time he went hunting rabbits with Sherry's father and brother: Crosby Broadwater and Crosby Broadwater Jr. "Sherry's daddy bought me a shotgun," Perry recalled. "He owns a whole lotta land. It was Christmas day and we were walking around and pretty soon a rabbit jumped up. Before I knew it, Crosby Jr. jumped up in the air and said, 'There goes a rabbit, there goes a rabbit.' Instead of him shooting the rabbit, he'd taken the gun and pointed it all around at everybody. Everybody was ducking and dodging."

It was enough to make Perry lose his appetite for hunting, if not for food. As a young boy he had already lost his right front tooth when an older cousin caught him flush in the mouth with a shot from a pellet gun at 50 yards. "I was lucky it didn't put my eye out," Perry said.

Much later, when he joined the Bears, several local dentists offered to replace the tooth free of charge. A "dunderheaded notion," wrote Chicago *Tribune* columnist Bernie Lincicome. "If Perry fills up the gap in his smile, how will we ever know if the light goes out when he closes his mouth?"

"Anyway," Perry said, "I don't mess with hunting no more unless I'm hunting for geese or something like that, something that flies. Or swims. I fish all the time." He credits the Broadwaters for teaching him to plumb the depths of Aiken's Lake Murray for crappie, bass and "whatever bites."

"I could stay fishing from sunup to sundown and if I don't catch none it's still fine," he said. "Fishing's nice. You can let your mind run. You can just let everything go and have fun."

Holiday barbecues at the Broadwaters were always a festive occasion. His inlaws would celebrate by roasting a whole pig. How much would William eat? "Shoot," he said. "Who knows? When I wasn't on a diet, I could go through three or four slabs of ribs real easy. Not too much meat on those bones."

Sherry had urged Perry to attend Michigan, which along with Michigan State, Auburn, Ohio State, Tennessee and UCLA had all entered the Perry recruiting derby for this touted athlete who had been named to the *Parade* All-American Prep team. Perry had averaged 18 points a game in basketball and was reportedly clocked at 11.4 in the 100-yard dash. But by now he knew he wanted to play professional football.

"It had been my goal ever since the fifth or sixth grade," he said. "Some people had come up to me and said, 'Do you know you can make

The Perry family gathers at their Aiken, S.C., home in the summer of 1984.

money doing what you like?' I said, 'No, I didn't know that.' They said, 'Those guys on TV playing pro ball, they get paid for that stuff.' I said, 'I'm gonna pursue that.'"

But Michigan was too far from home to suit Perry.

"Clemson's not big," Sherry countered.

"It's as big as Michigan or Michigan State," Perry answered.

Sherry said, "I didn't know that."

Finally Perry told her, "I'm going to Clemson [a two-hour drive from Aiken], where I can be close by you. If I go way up to Michigan, I'll never get to see you."

The recruiting process opened Perry's eyes to the real world of big-time college athletics. Asked if he ever received any "$150 handshakes" from overzealous boosters, he said "I'd rather not get into that."

"But look at Herschel Walker," he said. "Everybody said he didn't get anything at Georgia. Everybody knows that's different. But if you look at an athlete who comes from a poor family who doesn't have anything, he deserves something.

"I know I brought a lot of people into the games at Clemson. Any ballplayer ought to be getting at least $200 a month. That's not gonna hurt the university. Some players in college have moms and dads that have money. Most players, you know, they're black, and they don't have no money. That's the bottom line. You ought to have some money if you want to go out and buy a pair of jeans or something like that. Because people aren't going to give you anything."

Perry also knew early on he would return to Aiken after football was over. "No doubt about it," he said. "To tell you the truth I don't want to have to work after football. After all this is over I just want to relax and have some income and have fun."

11

Clemson's William "The Refrigerator" Perry measures up as an Outland Trophy, ° Lombardi Award Candidate

The celebrated Clemson poster that was a best-seller in Perry's senior year. The little guy in front of the poster is Jeremy Adams, whose father Al was a Clemson sports information aide.

THE CLEMSON TIGER

Clemson football player Ray Brown pushed the dormitory elevator button and waited. When the automatic doors finally slid open, he was speechless. Standing in front of him was a 285-pound freshman from Aiken—William Perry.

Brown blinked. Then he addressed his new teammate. "You're as big as a refrigerator," he said. "I'm going to call you 'GE.'"

By the time the 1981 season started the Clemson coaching staff had decided to utilize freshman Perry and 250-pound sophomore William Devane at nose guard on alternating series. They quickly developed the nickname, "The Bruise Brothers." But it wouldn't last.

Following a 13-3 victory in the third game over Herschel Walker and the fourth-ranked Georgia Bulldogs, Clemson sports information director Bob Bradley included this innocuous note in his weekly press release: "William Perry, Clemson's mammoth freshman nose guard from Aiken, has picked up a new nickname from his teammates. He's called 'GE' because of his resemblance to a refrigerator in size."

The rest is public relations history.

Against Georgia, Perry had recovered a Walker fumble that led to a Clemson touchdown. In the ninth game, second-ranked Clemson edged eighth-ranked North Carolina at Chapel Hill. It was the first time in Atlantic Coast Conference history two conference teams had taken top 10 rankings into the same game.

Perry had five tackles and two sacks against North Carolina to earn ACC Rookie-of-the-Week honors. *Sports Illustrated* mentioned his perform-ance and his nickname—GE. "I think that was the game I established myself," he said.

The Tigers became No. 1 in the rankings after completing their 11-0 regular season when Penn State upset top-ranked Pitt, 48-14. On January 1, 1982, Clemson secured the first national football championship in school history when the Tigers beat fourth-ranked Nebraska, 22-15, in the Orange Bowl. Perry, now playing at 305, and Devane effectively neutralized Nebraska center Dave Rimington. As a result, the Cornhuskers were not able to control the line of scrimmage.

Clemson finished the season ranked eighth in total defense, second in scoring defense and seventh in rushing defense. The Tigers were the only undefeated team in the nation. Even though Perry was only playing half the time, *Football News* named him to its first-team freshman All-American squad. Devane and Perry would continue to alternate at nose guard through Perry's junior year. During that time the Tigers won 30, lost two and tied two. No other Division I school had a better record during that period.

No. 66, Perry had the nickname "GE" before he became a generic refrigerator.

"I like the situation," said Devane after that championship season. "It means we both play about 35 or 40 plays a game. We know how much we're going to do, so we don't have to pace ourselves. We can cut loose."

Devane didn't hesitate to tutor his fellow Bruise Brother. "William's helped me along," said Perry. "I'd get real frustrated, but now I'm all right. William said, 'Don't worry, just do what you gotta do.' I'm enjoying it, but there's more work than I thought.'"

Meanwhile there was trouble in River City. Before the Orange Bowl the NCAA placed Clemson on two-year probation for recruiting violations that dated back to the Charley Pell era. The probation went into effect in November 1982 and lasted until November 1984.

The penalties: Clemson couldn't appear in a bowl game in 1982 or 1983; it was banned from television in 1983 and 1984. And the UPI poll deleted the Tigers from its rankings computers from 1982-84. In addition, the ACC prohibited the Tigers from accepting a bowl invitation in 1984. Pell had left in the late '70s. But coach Danny Ford's Tigers would pay the price.

Sports Illustrated quoted Perry as saying he didn't mind the bowl prohibition because he had already been to one. SI said Perry claimed the UPI ban was no problem because Clemson had already been No. 1. "But," Perry is supposed to have said, "I don't know if I can go two years without watching TV."

14

The summer after the national championship Perry and longtime steady Sherry Broadwater got married. "I had been coming home every weekend, every time I got a chance during my freshman year," said Perry. But the drive from Clemson to Aiken is a hard two hours. So he also called Sherry every night until he ran out of money. One month his phone bill totaled $600. Sherry scolded him. Perry's answer: "I love you, so I'm gonna call you."

He had even arranged his schedule so he had no classes on Thursdays. That allowed him a mid-week visit. He would drive to Aiken after Wednesday practice and be back at Clemson for late practice Thursday afternoon. "We won the national championship," said Perry. "But it was a tough year for me."

It wasn't as tough on Sherry. "I had all my family around," she said. "And I was taking classes. It wasn't that hard." But marriage made it easier. Late in the summer of 1982 Sherry presented her new husband with an eight-pound, four-ounce baby girl—Latavia Shenique Perry. William was ecstatic. "I was in the delivery room," he said. "When she came I just hollered. It's still a wonder."

Perry was 19 years old.

Clemson lost its first game to Georgia in 1982 and tied Doug Flutie and Boston College the next week. But the Tigers won their next nine in a row, including a 16-13 victory over 18th-ranked North Carolina at Chapel Hill. They followed that the next week with a 24-22 victory over powerful Maryland in which Perry had nine tackles.

The Tigers finished with a 9-1-1 record and a No. 8 ranking in the season-ending AP poll. AP named Perry to its third-team All-American squad. UPI and *Football News* accorded him honorable mention. *Football News* also named him its sophomore Defensive Player of the Year.

His weight had jumped to 310. But he never ceased to amaze his coaches and teammates with his athletic ability. Interestingly enough, Clem-

Perry's weightlifting paid off on the football field.

son defensive coordinator Tom Harper recommended Perry as an offensive weapon to other members of the coaching staff. Harper, who called Perry "P" for short, envisioned Perry in the backfield.

"Believe me when I said 'P' could pass better than Mike Eppley, who was our starting quarterback," Harper told Chicago *Sun-Times* columnist Ron Rapoport. "Believe me when I said he could punt better than Dale Hatcher [a third-round draft pick of the Los Angeles Rams]. Believe me when I said he could place-kick better than Donald Igwebuike [now playing for Tampa Bay]. Believe me when I said he could run better than any of our halfbacks.

"Hatcher was about as fine a punter as I've ever seen. But 'P' could kick it farther. He about kicked the air out of the ball. And 'P' could catch the ball as well as anybody we had. He'd line up at the end of practice and say, 'Hey, Harps, how do you want it? One-hand? Over the head?'"

And the Tigers practiced Perry at running back all the time. "We had another defensive lineman, just an ordinary person who weighed about 270," said Harper. "On Fridays when we didn't practice too hard, he and 'P' used to rehearse like a quarterback and a fullback. They'd run the option—drop back, sprint out. He was quicker than the guy we had at quarterback."

Perry even played defensive back in practice. "We had interception drills, tip drills—he'd do all of them," said Harper.

Harper said Perry could weigh 500 pounds and still look like an ordinary person because of his remarkable bone structure and sturdy musculature. "The thing I asked him is, 'How much longer can your ligaments and tendons last?' I told him you can last longer if you weigh what you're supposed to weigh."

But Perry had bulked up to 320 as a junior. The Tigers finished undefeated in the ACC and 9-1-1 overall. AP ranked them 11th at season's end. Their highlights were a 16-16 tie against 11th-ranked Georgia; a 16-3 victory at 10th-ranked North Carolina and a 52-27 drubbing of Maryland in their second-to-last game. More honors for Perry: AP first-team All-American; UPI first-team All-American; and Walter Camp first-team All-American.

The legend grew. When teammate Perry Tuttle offered to treat Perry to a meal at McDonald's, Perry accepted and reportedly ate $22 worth of Big Macs, fries, milk shakes and apple turnovers. All in one sitting. By the time Perry came back to Clemson for his senior year he weighed 335 pounds.

By now Devane had departed and the Clemson sports information office wanted to insure Perry would become the second unanimous All-American in the school's history. New York Giant safety Terry Kinard had been the first. When they received a phone call from Chicago graphics expert Jeff Pratt, a Clemson fan, they acted immediately.

Pratt's company, Sports Graphics, had used a 340 scanner to print large color separations of major league baseball players at a relatively small cost. On September 27, the Thursday before the Georgia Tech game, Clemson officials procured two refrigerators from Modern Supply in Williamston, South Carolina. Clemson photographer Lance McKinney spent an entire morning setting up a studio.

Brother Michael Dean was a Tiger who made William look like a relative lamb. ▶

The actual shoot took half an hour with a uniformed Perry striking more than 20 different poses in front of a refrigerator. "The photography was great and this enabled us to blow up the transparency 2,000 percent without losing a lot of quality," said Pratt.

The finished product arrived at Clemson October 19 at 1 P.M. The cost of the 4,000 posters: $10,000. The sports information department immediately shipped 2,000 of them to national media and high schools in Clemson's recruiting area. It took them 30 hours to sell out the remaining 2,000 to students and fans at $5 a crack. Ironically, when they sold the last poster at 6 P.M. after the October 20 Duke game, it was 60 years to the day after a Notre Dame publicity assistant named George Strickler had shot the famous "Four Horsemen" picture in South Bend, Indiana.

The poster gained national attention. "Clemson's William 'The Refrigerator' Perry measures up as an Outland Trophy & Lombardi Award Candidate," it read. But because the refrigerator used in the poster was not a General Electric, the Tiger staff revised history. Clemson's Perry was suddenly "The Refrigerator" even though many of his teammates continued to call him "GE."

The probation blues finally caught up to Clemson in 1984 and the Tigers slipped to 7-4. The Tigers won their first two games by a combined score of 95-7. But in the third game, Georgia's Kevin Butler, who would later become a teammate of Perry's with the Bears, kicked a 60-yard field goal with 11 seconds remaining to beat Clemson, 26-23. The Tigers also lost to Georgia Tech, 28-21; to Maryland, 41-23; and to South Carolina, 22-21, in the last game of Perry's collegiate career. The South Carolina defeat was the only one at home in Perry's four years.

But 1984 had been Perry's best year. It capped a college career that even included a 36-yard return of a blocked punt, the longest punt return by a Clemson player in four years. Perry also wound up as the all-time Clemson leader in "fumble involvement," causing or recovering 15 fumbles.

In 1984 he broke Dallas Cowboy tackle Randy White's all-time ACC record in tackles-for-loss in a season with 27 while also breaking the conference record for career quarterback sacks with 25. The list goes on and on.

At the 1984 Lombardi Award dinner, where Perry was a finalist, NBC announcer Dick Enberg was master of ceremonies and told Perry beforehand about his plans to have fun at Perry's expense. "Whenever you figure I've gone far enough, do whatever you want to me," Enberg told Perry. During the introduction he compared parts of Perry's body to parts of the refrigerator—the head was the freezer where they kept pralines and cream; the chest was for beer and milk; and the belly was for steaks, hamburgers and . . . And so on.

"Just after I mentioned three pounds of bacon," said Enberg, "he reached down, grabbed me by the belt and just lifted me over his head and held me there. He was so pleasant about it. And what made it wonderful was that it was the perfect thing for him to do."

At the Hula Bowl in January 1985, Perry was "absolutely the biggest player we've ever had," said executive director Mackay Yanagisawa. But it was time for the world's largest therapeutic recreation major to move on to bigger things. The NFL draft was approaching.

THE DRAFT

Chicago Bear personnel director Bill Tobin dropped the hints. But nobody caught on.

A week before the 1985 NFL draft in April a reporter called and wanted to know about this "Refrigerator" character from Clemson. Tobin grew animated. He talked about how much weight Perry had lost since the end of his senior year at Clemson. He talked about having visited with Perry's college coaches and how they had raved about him.

But the reporter only wanted to know whether Perry was a nose tackle or a regular defensive tackle. Tobin said he could play both positions. When another reporter visited Tobin for a pre-draft briefing in his second-floor office at Halas Hall, Tobin actually pulled a picture of Perry out of his desk and showed it the same way a father shows a snapshot of a son.

But nobody suspected a thing. The Bears had made it clear they were interested in defensive line help even though they had set a league record with 72 sacks in 1984. Starting tackles Dan Hampton, a former All-Pro, and reliable Steve McMichael had played major roles in the NFL's No. 1 defense. But both had knee histories.

The savants figured the Bears would take either Notre Dame's Mike Gann or Southern Mississippi's Richard Byrd, both defensive linemen. Both were still available Tuesday morning when the time came for the Bears to select 22nd on the first round.

But the debate that raged in the Bears' draft "War Room" next to Tobin's office revolved around Perry and Florida State wide receiver Jesse Hester. General manager Jerry Vainisi and team president Michael McCaskey weren't totally sold on Perry. But Tobin and Ditka convinced them. Significantly, defensive coordinator Buddy Ryan was absent.

At a press conference moments later Tobin freely conceded the Bears had taken a chance. "No guts, no glory," he said. "He's got a chance to be a very dominating player. He's also got a chance, if he doesn't control his weight, of making us all look bad. We're betting on his character, that he can keep the weight off. But we're aware that it's a risk."

Al Davis' Los Angeles Raiders, who reportedly would have chosen Perry with the 23rd pick, settled for Hester. Within minutes, ESPN-TV analysts Paul Zimmerman and Paul Maguire were ridiculing the Bears' choice of Perry. "Do they still have the stockyards in Chicago?" asked one. "Maybe the postmaster will give Perry his own zip code," cracked the other.

Ditka was watching the broadcast and became furious. Eventually he calmed down and explained what had sold him on a player the Bear scouts had weighed at 358 pounds and clocked in a lumbering 5.36 40-yard dash just three months earlier.

"I hate to think of him going somewhere else," said Ditka. "If you think about lining up to play Minnesota or Green Bay or even San Francisco, the

Perry meets the media at Bear headquarters following his first-round selection in the draft.

first thing we're going to do is not say, 'How do we block Fred Dean or Ezra Johnson?' It's 'What are we going to do about that big guy in the middle?' Do you go around him? Do you run wide all the time? Do you dare go right at him?

"I guarantee you they're going to have to double-team him. That will free up Richard Dent or Dan Hampton to go one-on-one. I think Perry could have the impact of a 'Big Daddy' Lipscomb."

Perry paid no attention to ESPN. And by the time the dust had settled in Aiken ("The noise just about blew the roof off when we heard I was picked in the first round."), Perry was on board a jet for an afternoon introduction to the Chicago media.

Wearing a size-60 blazer and a natty golf cap, Perry announced his current weight at 317 pounds. Several "Honey Bear" cheerleaders, serving as draft day hostesses at Halas Hall, put their hands over their mouths and giggled when Perry walked into the press room. At a pre-draft scouting combine meeting two months earlier, Perry had stepped on a scale and pegged it at its limit of 350 pounds. "William Perry, Clemson," announced the scale operator. "350 and still rising."

Perry answered an unending stream of questions about his weight. He described a typical meal as "three, four chickens, no problem, ribs." And he smiled his gap-toothed smile. He had been rehearsing for this day all his life. "I feel sorry for the centers who are going to have to face him," said Ditka. "Including ours."

Then somebody held up a new No. 72 Bears jersey with Perry's name on the back. "He'll look good in that navy uniform, or two uniforms, whatever we put on him," Ditka added.

By midseason in 1985, Buffalo defensive end Bruce Smith, the first player picked April 30, was still struggling. Houston cornerback Richard Johnson, the 11th player taken, was a certified bust. And only Cincinnati wide receiver Eddie Brown was having anything close to Perry's impact.

The first 10 linemen chosen averaged 267 pounds. Perry was the biggest. "I wasn't surprised the Bears took him," said Cleveland personnel director Bill Davis. "It took two men to block him in college. He's that strong." The ESPN experts were strangely silent.

THE ORIGINAL MONSTERS

George Halas, the Papa Bear, was with the Bears for more than 60 years as player, coach and owner.

It's hard to imagine the late George S. Halas ever being 25 years old. But there he was in Canton, Ohio, on September 17, 1920, representing the Decatur (Ill.) Staleys in a meeting attended by officials from 12 other football teams. The place was Ralph Hay's Hupmobile showroom. The young, jut-jawed Halas sat on a fender.

The price for admission to the American Professional Football Association that later grew into the wildly-successful National Football League: $100. The Staleys shut out 12 of their 13 opponents that year, losing only to the Chicago Cardinals, 7-6. Each player earned $1,900 for the season.

In 1922 Halas moved the Staleys from Decatur to Chicago. One year later he renamed them the Chicago Bears. When Harold (Red) Grange signed with the Bears for $100,000 on November 22, 1925, professional football was a sport about to become a business.

Grange had been a sensation at the University of Illinois, Halas' alma mater. They called Grange "The Galloping Ghost." Sixty years later Chicago *Sun-Times* sportswriter Kevin Lamb would call a 310-pound Bear rookie named William Perry "The Galloping Roast."

The idea was to expose the rest of the country to Grange. Halas took the Bears on a whirlwind, 16-game, coast-to-coast tour that began

Red Grange, "The Galloping Ghost," starred at the University of Illinois before launching a distinguished pro career as a Bear.

Bronko Nagurski, one of the original Monsters, made a remarkable comeback at the age of 35.

November 26 and ended January 31. In his first game Grange gained only 36 yards in a 0-0 tie with the Chicago Cardinals before 36,000 curiosity seekers at Wrigley Field. Two weeks later 73,000 New Yorkers showed up at the Polo Grounds to see Grange run back an interception 30 yards for a touchdown that helped beat the Giants, 19-7.

Grange was the first star in a Chicago Bear galaxy that grew as the popularity of the league grew.

After Grange came Bronislau (Bronko) Nagurski. Nagurski was born in Rainy River, Ontario, to Ukranian parents. He was an All-American fullback and tackle at the University of Minnesota and came to personify the "Monsters of the Midway" tag later hung on the Bears. In 1934 his blocking enabled Beattie Feathers to become the first 1,000-yard running back in NFL history. Nagurski finished his pro career with 2,778 yards rushing and became a charter member of the Professional Football Hall of Fame in 1963.

In 1939 the Bears traded an end named "Eggs" Manske to Pittsburgh

22

for the right to choose Columbia quarterback Sid Luckman with the second pick of the draft. Luckman had been a fun-loving, single-wing, Ivy League tailback with no great regard for professional football. So Halas first had to convince him to turn pro, then he had to sell him on the merits of the revolutionary T-formation. Luckman tripped over his own feet the first time he ever took a practice snap in the T-formation. But in 1943 he became the first NFL quarterback to pass for more than 400 yards in one game. Seven of his passes that day resulted in Bear touchdowns.

Luckman lasted 12 years in the NFL, completing 904 of 1,744 passes for 14,686 yards and 139 touchdowns. The Hall of Fame inducted him in 1965. In later years he grew increasingly close to Halas as a friend, advisor and confidante. He was crushed when Halas died in the fall of 1983.

The tight end on Halas' last championship team was fierce Mike Ditka. Symbolically, Ditka was to the 1963 Bears what Nagurski had been to the prewar team. Not coincidentally, Halas' last major move before his death was to install Ditka as his head coach.

Ditka had been a tight end, a defensive end, a middle linebacker and a punter at Pitt. And the Bears made him their first-round draft choice in 1961. He caught 75 passes in 1964, an NFL record for tight ends until San Diego's Kellen Winslow grabbed 89 in 1980.

"I was in charge of drafting for the Bears when I drafted Mike for the team," said George Allen, Halas' chief lieutenant in 1963. "He hadn't caught a lot of passes, but I thought he might make a perfect tight end—and I was right. Almost from the start he was better than others at the position. He was an excellent blocker; he seldom missed. He was an excellent receiver; he seldom missed. He was big and very strong and extremely difficult to bring down. He broke tackles and ran over people."

Mike Ditka, a first-round draft choice out of Pittsburgh in 1961, was on the Bears' last championship team in 1963. He returned as head coach in 1981 to lead Chicago back into championship contention.

Gale Sayers set all sorts of records, once scoring six touchdowns in a game.

If Ditka ran over people, Gale Sayers ran by people. The Bears acquired Sayers in the same 1965 draft that produced Hall of Fame linebacker Dick Butkus and Pro Bowl wide receiver Dick Gordon.

Sayers was a slashing, instinctive runner who scored six touchdowns in one game in the mud at Wrigley Field late in his rookie season. Before injuries ended his career prematurely in 1971, Sayers won two NFL rushing titles, set six league records and 16 Bear marks.

"When he was going wide and found a crowd, he was the best at reversing his field and getting loose," said Allen. "I wish he'd lasted longer. I'm grateful he lasted as long as he did."

Injuries also shortened the football career of Butkus, who according to Allen, "played with the ferocity of an angered animal." Butkus' off-the-field personality was even a match for the hard-nosed Halas.

Ditka had once credited Halas with "throwing nickels around like manhole covers" in contract talks. Butkus understood what Ditka was talking about in 1965 when he tried to play off an AFL offer against the Bears in search of more money.

But Halas knew Butkus had played his high school football at Chicago

Vocational before attending Illinois. He knew Butkus didn't want to leave home. Initially, Butkus took his frustrations out on his new teammates.

"I recall clearly that on his first day of practice with the Bears, Butkus was knocking down his own teammates left and right," recalled Allen. "Veterans like Doug Atkins vowed to get even with him. But throughout his career, players were always vowing to get even with Butkus. No one ever did.

"Butkus always got the better of every player he ever faced. He scared people and nothing ever scared him. I hate to say this, but I think he enjoyed hurting people. He really enjoyed playing."

According to the story that made the rounds at Illinois when Butkus played there, he would stay home and cry when weather canceled practice; he couldn't hit anybody that day.

There were many other memorable Bears. The Hall of Fame has since inducted 14 other ex-Bear players: defensive end Doug Atkins, quarterback-kicker George Blanda, tackle-linebacker George Connor, halfback Paddy Driscoll, guard Danny Fortmann, linebacker Bill George, tackle Ed Healey, end Bill Hewitt, tackle Roy (Link) Lyman, halfback George McAfee, tackle-guard George Musso, tackle Joe Stydahar, center George Trafton and center-linebacker Clyde (Bulldog) Turner.

All-Pro Bear greats have included fullback Bill Osmanski, end Ken Kavanaugh, quarterback Johnny Lujack, end Harlan Hill, fullback Rick Casares, defensive end Ed Sprinkle, special teamer J.C. Caroline, flanker Johnny Morris, linebacker Larry Morris, linebacker Doug Buffone, center Mike Pyle, linebacker Joe Fortunato and defensive back Richie Petitbon.

The history is rich and too deep to dismiss in passing. But let the record show the Bears won the NFL's first championship game on

Dick Butkus was an awesome linebacker from the University of Illinois who made it to the Pro Football Hall of Fame.

25

Bear quarterback Carl Brumbaugh carries against the Giants in the first NFL championship game in 1933. Chicago, the home team, won, 23-21.

December 17, 1933, in front of 26,000 people at Wrigley Field. Boston Redskin owner George Preston Marshall had brought about this game when he demanded the league be split into divisions.

So the Bears, champions of the West, defeated the Giants, champions of the East, 23-21. "Automatic" Jack Manders kicked three field goals and two extra points. Before the game somebody asked Giants' coach Steve Owen how you stopped the 238-pound Nagurski. "With a shotgun," Owen replied.

But the Bears' heroes that day were an end named Bill Hewitt, who refused to wear a helmet, and Bill Karr. Late in the game Nagurski hit Hewitt with a jump pass for 14 yards. Before the Giants could bring him down, Hewitt lateraled to Karr, who covered the remaining 19 for the winning touchdown. The winning shares were $210.23 apiece.

The following year the Giants turned the tables in the famous "Sneakers Game." Trailing 10-3 at halftime, they switched from football shoes to basketball shoes early in the final quarter for better traction on the frozen Polo Grounds' turf.

The Bears increased their lead to 13-3 after three periods. But the comeback began when tailback Ed Danowski threw a 28-yard touchdown pass to Ike Frankian. That cut the lead to 13-10. New York went on to outscore the Bears, 27-0, in the final period and capture its first title, 30-13.

The Giants would have donned the basketball shoes earlier, but a subway messenger named Abe Cohen didn't arrive from Manhattan College with the crucial brogans until the fourth period. The Giants called time out with 10 minutes to play, rushed to the sidelines, changed shoes and promptly changed NFL history.

The Bears returned to the championship game in 1937. Again it was cold (15 degrees), and again the field was icy. But this time the opponent was the Washington Redskins and the site was the friendly confines of Wrigley Field. It didn't matter.

Behind rookie quarterback Sammy Baugh, the Redskins outscored the Bears, 14-0, in the final period to win, 28-21. The winning drive covered 80 yards in 11 plays, Baugh hitting Ed Justice for the game-winning 35-yard touchdown pass. Baugh had frozen the Bear secondary with a pump-fake to end Charles Malone that freed Justice.

But the Bears would have their revenge three years later. During the 1940 regular season the Redskins had beaten the Bears again, 7-3. The championship game figured to be a classic with Luckman matching Baugh pass for pass.

A clue to the outcome of the game came during the train ride from Chicago to Washington. "Most of the time when a team rides a train, the boys play cards or read or hold bull sessions," Luckman would say later. "But this ride was different. There weren't five words spoken on the whole trip. Then we got off the train and the Washington papers called us crybabies and front-runners."

The Redskins had just finished a three-hour workout the day before the game when the Bears arrived for their practice. Washington running back Andy Farkas remembers coming out of the shower room just as the Bears stepped on the field. "They came out screaming like a pack of wild Indians," said Farkas. "They took off and ran the length of the field. They circled the goal posts and started back, and they were still screaming."

Halas turned to assistant Hunk Anderson and remarked, "My, but the boys are enthusiastic. Get them back inside. I don't want them to lose that kind of enthusiasm." The Bears did not practice that day.

On the second play of the game Bill Osmanski swept left end for 68 yards and a touchdown. The Redskins answered Osmanski's score with a drive that died when a Baugh pass was dropped in the end zone. The Bears scored three touchdowns in the first 12 minutes and 10 seconds. And a rout was on.

By the end of this 73-0 slaughter, Halas was mercifully ordering his team to run for extra points. The equipment manager at Griffith Stadium, if no one else, appreciated the gesture. The Redskins were running out of footballs.

Willie Wilkin of the Redskins stops the Bears' Bill Osmanski in this instance, but Chicago hit the jackpot, 73-0, to win the NFL crown in 1940.

27

After the game Baugh was asked if he thought things would have been different if his first-quarter pass hadn't been dropped in the end zone. "Yes," Baugh said, "The score might have been 73-7."

The next day the Bears had officially become "The Monsters of the Midway." It was a nickname initially coined to describe Amos Alonzo Stagg's University of Chicago teams. Nobody complained when the Bears expropriated it by default.

The Bears returned to defend their title against the New York Giants the following year. The game was played two weeks after Japan's attack on Pearl Harbor. Only 13,341 fans were at Wrigley Field on a balmy 47-degree Sunday afternoon. Tickets ranged in price from $2.20 to $4.40.

By halftime the Bears were ahead, but in a way that was almost embarrassing for a team with their talent. The Bears had run off 53 offensive plays compared to only 10 for the Giants and it was a bald-headed placekicker named Bob Snyder who kicked three field goals to give Chicago its 6-3 lead at intermission.

But Norm Standlee, scoring twice, and George McAfee and Ken Kavanaugh, one each, led the way in the second half for a 37-9 victory.

Less than a month later, many Bears marched off to war. Lieutenant Commander George Halas was among the first to go.

It was back to Griffith Stadium in 1942 for a title re-match with the humiliated but talented Redskins. McAfee, Kavanaugh and Standlee were off fighting the war, and Osmanski and Joe Stydahar needed furloughs to get to the game. A key play was a Baugh interception in the end zone. Washington won, 14-6.

The seesaw teetered back in the Bears favor in 1943 when the Bears avenged the avengers with a 41-21 title victory over the Redskins at Wrigley

Warming up for their 41-21 victory over the Redskins in the 1943 championship game was the Bears' backfield (from left) of Dante Magnani, Harry Clark, Bronko Nagurski and Sid Luckman.

Field. With Halas in the Navy, Hunk Anderson was running the team. Luckman was never better, throwing five touchdown passes. The sentimental hero was the 35-year-old Nagurski, who had retired five years earlier but returned because war losses had depleted the Bears' ranks. To add insult to injury, a policeman refused to allow Washington owner George Preston Marshall to visit his team's locker room at halftime.

Pro football had started as a game and turned into a business. But it didn't really become an entertainment form until WW II ended. New cars were rolling off the assembly lines and 58,346 people showed up at the Polo Grounds on December 15, 1946, to see Luckman lead the Bears past the Giants, 24-14.

But a scandal cast a pall over their victory. Before the game a small-time gambler named Alvin Paris told authorities he had offered bribes to Giant fullback Merle Hapes and quarterback Frankie Filchock. Both refused the bribe, but both failed to report the offer. The story broke in the New York papers.

On the eve of the game Hapes finally admitted Paris' offer. Filchock still denied it. NFL commissioner Bert Bell said Hapes couldn't play and Filchock could. Filchock's own fans booed him from the outset. Early in the game he broke his nose. Bell later suspended both players.

It was 10 years, 1956, before the Bears returned to another league championship game. Luckman and Nagurski had long since retired. The Giants, led by Alex Webster, Frank Gifford, Charlie Conerly and Kyle Rote, routed the Bears at Yankee Stadium, 47-7.

One paragraph in the Bears' 1985 press guide is delightfully succinct in summing up the Bears' 14-10 win over the Giants in the 1963 championship game: "The temperature was 11 but the Bear defense was hot, intercepting five passes, two setting up TDs. QB Y.A. Tittle played the second half with a strained knee incurred on a tackle by Bear LB Larry Morris."

The Giants led, 10-7, in the third period when a Tittle screen pass found its way into the paws of lumbering Bear defensive end Ed O'Bradovich. O'Bradovich shambled 10 yards to the Giant 14.

"I kept running and running," said the 255-pound O'Bradovich. "I wanted to score a touchdown." But the farther he ran, the farther apart the white lines kept getting. Not to worry. Five plays later Bear quarterback Bill Wade negotiated two yards into the end zone and the Bears had all the points they needed.

During the previous summer O'Bradovich had developed a strep throat that turned into something worse. And the doctors couldn't diagnose the complication. "Sure," he said. "I was scared."

But he got well. So did the Bears.

There have been many other milestones in Bear history apart from the legends and the championships. In 1934 Halas founded "Halas University," the Bears' alumni association that celebrates annually with a homecoming party. In 1941 their fight song, "Bear Down Chicago Bears," was published.

On October 22, 1961, the Bear defense solved San Francisco coach Red Hickey's vaunted shotgun offense and trounced the 49ers, 31-0. In 1967 Halas retired from coaching. And two years later, an overmatched young coach named Jim Dooley led the Bears to a 1-13 season.

Perhaps the most touching story in Bear history was unfolding at the same time. Brian Piccolo was a longshot running back from Wake Forest

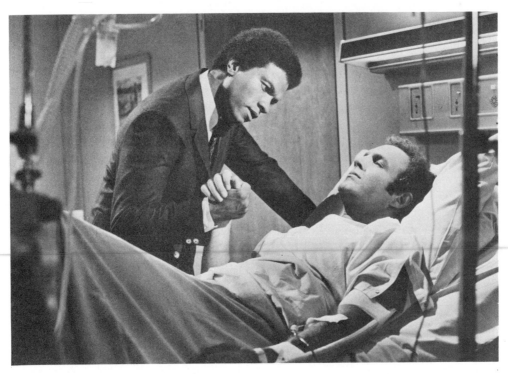

James Caan, playing the late Chicago Bear fullback Brian Piccolo, gets support from Billy Dee Williams (Gale Sayers) in *Brian's Song*.

who played four years with the Bears before dying of cancer June 16, 1970. He was immensely popular with his teammates and especially close to Gale Sayers.

Piccolo's courage in the face of death inspired *A Short Season*, a book about his struggle by Jeannie Morris, wife of former Bear wide receiver Johnny Morris. Piccolo's story evolved into a made-for-TV movie entitled *Brian's Song*, starring James Caan and Billy Dee Williams.

Piccolo died at the age of 26 and left a wife and three young daughters behind. "Pic was a fan's ballplayer, a coach's ballplayer, but above all a ballplayer's ballplayer," wrote Morris in the foreword of his wife's book. The team later established the Piccolo Fund that has since raised more than a million dollars in the fight against cancer.

Opponents had respected Piccolo's braveness, too, partially because the Bears had always grudgingly returned the respect when deserved. One of the more curious Bear opponents over the years was a 6-3, 350-pound Detroit middle guard named Les Bingaman. Bingaman toiled for the Lions from 1948 to 1954. The former Illinois guard played the nose in the Lions' famed "Eagle 8 Defense."

But most people have long since forgotten the role he played as a precursor to William Perry. "I used to use him in the backfield," recalled former Lion quarterback Bobby Layne. "Buddy [Lion coach Parker] didn't like it very well, but he let me use him. We never took it seriously. I handed off to Bing a few times and he scored a touchdown in an exhibition game."

The Lions later utilized 6-4, 250-pound tight end Leon Hart as a fullback in short-yardage situations. And when San Francisco coach Bill Walsh placed 264-pound guard Guy McIntyre in the 49er backfield during the 1984 NFC championship game, the light bulb of an idea that would switch on a whole country had been screwed firmly into place. The Bears lost that day, 23-0. But Ditka would gain his measure of revenge less than a year later.

SURROUNDED BY BEARS

The ballyhooed contract William Perry finally signed with the Bears in August called for a reported $1.356 million over four years. But it was laden with so much fine print and so many weight clauses, that it read like the Rosetta Stone.

The Bears would pay Perry approximately $340,000 a year. But roughly $108,000 per annum would be tied, like a millstone, to his weight. During the regular season the Bears would weigh Perry every Tuesday and Friday. Each time he came in under the prescribed weight it would be worth $1,000 in his paycheck.

Meanwhile they would test him for stamina and body fat percentage six times a year. Each passing grade would be worth an added $6,000. Additional incentives were designed to keep tabs on Perry in the offseason. They would be worth $40,000 if met.

"It's totally unique and there will never be anything like this again," said Bear general manager Jerry Vainisi of the contract. "We wanted to try to give him the money that a first-rounder would get, but only if he earned it by keeping in shape." After 10 regular-season games Perry had missed the prescribed weight only once.

William Perry works out at the Bears' preseason minicamp in Lake Forest in May 1985.

31

But prolonged contract negotiations forced him to report late to the Bears' summer training camp in Platteville, Wisconsin, a small college town in remote southwestern Wisconsin. He had gained 17 pounds since the draft and his weight had soared back into the 330s. To be sure, this was still the manchild who wore a size-61 sports jacket, triple extra-large shirt with a 23-inch neck, 48-waist pants and size-22 finger ring at Clemson.

The Bears had tried to put Perry on a special diet after the draft. But when contract talks with St. Louis-based agent Jim Steiner hardened, they had lost touch.

Now it was early August and the relentless summer sun was beating a tattoo on Perry's ample body. One writer called Perry "The Admiral of Avoirdupois." On the second day of workouts, he missed the afternoon practice because of the heat. Head coach Mike Ditka had sharp words for Perry. But defensive coordinator Buddy Ryan stung the rookie even harder.

"He's a wasted draft pick," said Ryan, a native Oklahoman who raises Kentucky thoroughbreds in the offseason. "He's a nice kid, but so's my son, and I wouldn't want him playing for me." Ryan, outspoken as the day is long, was upset the Bears hadn't reached terms with holdout starting linebacker Al Harris and holdout All-Pro safety Todd Bell. He suggested the Bears would have been better ignoring Perry and spending their money on Harris or Bell. Then Ryan called Perry "Fat Boy" in front of his teammates.

Suddenly Perry was a cause celebre for all the wrong reasons. But he didn't panic. And he didn't pout when the Bears barred him from their training table food line. Every evening after two-a-day practices the Bears would pile into the commons and load their plates with steaks, chicken, lobster, ribs, mashed potatoes, gravy, ice cream and cookies. Perry's tray, sprinkled with carrots, celery, watermelon and assorted other rabbit food, was brought to him.

Meanwhile Ryan's remarks sparked an angry response from Bear personnel director Bill Tobin. "I've been confident from the day we drafted him that Perry was an excellent football player," said Tobin later. "The thing that got me upset was when someone in our organization took a cheap shot at him. Then you've got to stand up and say something."

Reserve defensive lineman Tyrone Keys sympathized with Perry and the two became close. "I've been called all these names all my life," Perry told Keys. "There isn't anything they can call me that I haven't heard before." Perry was also beginning to suspect what many other Bears already knew: Ryan had a method to his madness.

Ryan had insisted middle linebacker Mike Singletary was too short as a rookie. Singletary responded by going to the Pro Bowl two years later. Ryan had labeled outside linebacker Wilber Marshall, the Bears' first-round pick in 1984, a "baby." Marshall responded by growing into Harris' spot and making people wonder how they had ever gotten along without him.

Soon the pounds began dripping off Perry's massive body and the double practice sessions stopped being a daily torture. Perry said he had once lost 22 pounds in one day during preseason practice in 115-degree heat at Clemson. Asked if he ever tired of the endless questions about his weight, Perry replied in a friendly South Carolina accent: "Lessen you get tired of asking."

In a team meeting, Ryan told Perry he wanted him to be more than a refrigerator. "I want you to be a refrigerator on wheels," Ryan said. Then he

Like every Chicago rooter, coach Mike Ditka had a singular goal: A return to the championship days of yore.

cussed Perry for running the wrong way on a "twist" pass rush. "Sorry, coach," said the unfailingly good-natured Perry, "one of my wheels fell off." Even Ryan smiled.

The Bears opened their preseason August 9 with a 10-3 loss to the Cardinals in the wilting heat of St. Louis' Busch Stadium. Regular Bear tackle Dan Hampton was still recovering from offseason knee surgery so Ryan played Perry the first 50 minutes of the game. "Just to make it through that is a feat in itself," said Bear guard Kurt Becker.

During the third period Ryan told Perry he wouldn't be allowed on the team plane back to Platteville if he didn't produce a quarterback sack. "So I got one," said Perry. The sack occurred early in the fourth period when Perry chased down Cardinal quarterback Kyle Mackey. When he got back to the sidelines Ryan greeted Perry with an uncharacteristic high five.

"He's still young and he's got quite a lot to learn," said Cardinal guard Doug Dawson after the game. "But I didn't knock him off the ball any. If he's got a weakness it's that he's mostly a power rusher. He tries to knock you into the quarterback. That might not get him too many sacks."

Hampton's absence for most of the preseason proved a blessing in disguise. It enabled Perry to log more playing time than he might have otherwise. But his progress was still slow. Part of the problem was Ryan's complex defensive system. Another part of the problem was still Perry's weight and stamina. Hampton insisted he looked "a biscuit shy of 350." Hence, the nickname "Biscuit." Other Bears referred to Perry unflatteringly as "Mudslide."

"I would say he's a year away and he's going to have to pay a heck of a price," said Ryan a week before the regular-season opener against Tampa

33

Record-setting Walter Payton set the all-time NFL rushing mark in 1984 and was launching his 11th season in 1985.

Bay. The Bears had other problems. Ditka wasn't concerned so much about their 1-3 preseason record as he was with the continued absence of Bell and Harris. Hampton's knee was still slow in responding, Walter Payton was going into his 11th year and fragile quarterback Jim McMahon still hadn't completed an entire NFL season without injury.

Many experts said the Bears would be lucky to repeat their 10-6 NFC Central championship year of 1984. Nobody dreamed they would win their first 10 games. And nobody could have known the role Perry would play in their quick rise to national prominence. But everybody knew the key personalities would have to be Payton, McMahon and Ditka.

Ryan's defense had led the NFL in fewest yards allowed in 1984 while setting a league record for sacks with 72. The Bears would miss Bell and Harris. But their personnel—led by Singletary, Hampton, veteran safety Gary Fencik, outside linebacker Otis Wilson and the incorrigible Steve McMichael—was superior. Plus, their complex scheme was often indecipherable to opponents.

Payton had broken Jim Brown's all-time NFL rushing record of 12,312 yards against the Saints in the sixth game of the 1984 season. President Reagan phoned afterward. Payton told him to "Say hi to Nancy." It was a memorable afternoon.

34

In the locker room later, Payton's high school coach, Charles Boston, stood off to the side while Payton dealt with an army of reporters. Boston quietly remembered the late summer of 1970, the first year of legally enforced integration in Jackson, Mississippi.

Boston's Columbia Wildcats were playing nearby Prentiss High School. Because of the new law, Boston and 20 of his players had transferred to Columbia from all-black Jefferson High. Sixteen whites had remained. Columbia won when Payton skittered 95 and 65 yards for two touchdowns. But the victory was much bigger than eight points.

"That did it for integration," said Boston. "The people didn't see a black boy running down the field. They saw a Columbia High School Wildcat."

Payton never stopped integrating. He had integrated his strength and speed to become the best all-around running back in anybody's memory. "You couldn't help but notice him," said Bill Tobin of the first time he saw Payton. "He looked like a Greek God. Even in street clothes." And Jackson State's Payton had integrated his impish personality into a team that before his arrival in 1975 had practiced an offense vs. defense segregation almost as invidious as what Payton had helped conquer in Mississippi.

He only missed one game in 10 years of NFL beatings. And he gained 13,309 yards on 3,047 carries in that span. The only goal he hadn't achieved was playing on a championship team. Many of his teammates wanted it more for him than they did for themselves. "He's a good, down-to-earth person, a humble person by nature," said running mate Matt Suhey, the Bears' starting fullback. "He's very appreciative of the people around him. He doesn't want anybody to dislike him, and I don't think there's one guy on the team who does." But the preseason doubters pointed to Payton's age—31—and wondered about his legs.

If Payton's lyrical influence on the Bears was a sweet inspiration, McMahon was a combination Springsteen rocker and heavy metal—all dark shades, punk haircuts and leers—beer for breakfast and cornerbacks for lunch. A *Pittsburgh Press* headline proclaimed him: "THE NEW BOBBY LAYNE." The subhead read: "McMahon, free-flinger, humdinger, TD-slinger." And if he happened to turn up on the cover of *Rolling Stone* on the way to the Super Bowl, that would be just fine, too.

As a Roman Catholic at predominantly Mormon Brigham Young University, McMahon had set NCAA Division I passing and total offense records. But he was constantly at odds with the school's hierarchy. "I'm not a Mormon and I don't believe in what they believe in," he said bluntly. "That's one reason I didn't get along too well there. That's the way they are and this is the way I am. I wasn't trying to push it down anybody's throat that I was doing something wrong. I had different beliefs. Why try to change just because you're somewhere where everybody else is like they are?"

"He IS like Bobby Layne," said general manager Jerry Vainisi, comparing McMahon to the former Detroit and Pittsburgh quarterback. "He drinks like Bobby Layne. He throws like Bobby Layne." But his idol on and off the field was former Jet quarterback Joe Namath.

McMahon, like the hell-raising Layne, did not possess an especially strong arm. But his release was quick, his feet were quicker and his presence on the field was quicker yet. His bravado was the tragic flaw that cost him the second half of 1984 and almost his career. The injury occurred in the 10th game, a brutally physical 17-6 victory over the defending Super Bowl champion Raiders at Chicago's Soldier Field.

35

Free-wheeling quarterback Jim McMahon sported a shaved head at training camp.

While scrambling for extra yards, McMahon exposed himself to a vicious one-two hit from Raider tackle Bill Pickel and linebacker Jeff Barnes. Doctors eventually diagnosed it as a lacerated kidney. It was dangerously close to a ruptured kidney that would have meant no more football.

McMahon didn't play again in 1984. Former Chiefs' quarterback Steve Fuller replaced him and performed admirably. But the Bears sorely missed McMahon in the NFC championship game, a 23-0 San Francisco shutout. In the offseason Ditka insisted McMahon would be a more judicious scrambler in 1985.

At the Brian Piccolo golf tournament in the summer of '85 McMahon showed up wearing a tank-top, cutoff jeans and a pair of flip-flops with spikes. In Platteville he rode around training camp on a motor scooter looking like a stunt man from the cast of the apocalyptic Mel Gibson movie *The Road Warrier*. McMahon never tried to hide his disdain for playbooks, meetings and film study.

But underneath it all was the same burning, competitive fire that kept Ditka's pilot light going. "Jim is also like a young Ditka," said Vainisi. "They are both intense. Maybe Ditka is a little bit more intense off the field. Jim works hard, but he likes to party. We would rather have the normal types, but Jim gets the job done. If you're winning, you stay with it, and Jim wins a high percentage of his games."

Bear president Michael McCaskey, Halas' oldest grandson, had extended Ditka's contract the week before the NFC championship game. And that was part of the reason the subsequent 1-3 preseason record didn't faze him. Ditka was more concerned with tuning an offense that had only averaged 20 points per game in 1984 and refining the concepts he had brought from Dallas. After his playing career ended in 1972, he had served nine years as a Tom Landry Cowboy assistant. And it always bothered him how his emotions would breakdance with his heart every time the Cowboys played the Bears. "It seemed funny seeing that uniform and playing or coaching against it," he said.

When it became clear that an ailing Halas would dismiss incumbent coach Neill Armstrong after a miserable 6-10 season in 1981, Ditka wrote Halas a letter outlining why he was the man for the job. Halas listened and hired him January 20, 1982, just two weeks after Armstrong's firing.

"Mike is a blend of both the Lombardi simplicity and the multiple offense where coaching is today," said Landry. "He complemented me personally to a large extent. He was always a believer in giving a player a job and letting him get it done."

Many observers thought the Bears had gotten the wrong Landry assistant. They preferred the cerebral Dan Reeves to the headstrong Ditka the same way Mario Puzo's Godfather trusted the family business to shrewd son Michael Corleone instead of the impetuous Sonny. But Reeves was already at Denver and the Godfather logic didn't do justice to Ditka as an Xs and Os man. Every time he threw a clipboard or punched out a locker, one more person forgot how far he had brought the Bear offense in such a short period of time.

When a *Sports Illustrated* poll of 200 NFL players listed Ditka tied with Shula behind Landry as the coach they'd least like to play for, Ditka said he was "flattered."

"Probably those 200 players couldn't play for Tom, Don or I," he said. "They're probably lazy butts who wouldn't want to pay the price. I can understand *me*. But a guy who would say he wouldn't want to play for Landry or Shula has got to be a lazy bum."

Could Ditka have played for Ditka? "Yeah. Because I want to win. That's the only thing I want to do. If a player wants to win, he should have no problem. If he wants to be patted on the butt every time he does something wrong, then he'll have a problem."

So Ditka set about surrounding himself with those kinds of people, especially on offense. The first chore was in the offensive line where no Bear had played in the Pro Bowl since center Mike Pyle, a Ditka teammate, in 1964.

One of his first moves was to switch defensive lineman Mark Bortz, a rookie in 1983, to offensive line. Bortz' 6-6, 269-pound frame, distinguished by huge arms and great leverage, was prototypical of the new offensive linemen to whom the rules had granted unheard-of freedom to grab and hold. Bortz soon earned Noah Jackson's starting left guard spot. His teammates called him "Bortzilla."

And he was the perfect complement to left tackle Jimbo Covert, an agile strongman from Pitt, Ditka's alma mater. Covert was the Bears' No. 1 choice in 1983. And behind him and Bortz, the Bears became a "lefthanded" running team. Center Jay Hilgenberg, nephew of former Viking linebacker Wally Hilgenberg, had done nothing but improve in five years. And the Bears were solid, if unspectacular, on the right side of the line with

37

guard Kurt Becker, tackle Keith Van Horne and above-average backups Tom Thayer and Andy Frederick.

In the backfield there was McMahon, the nonpareil Payton and the underrated Suhey. Emery Moorehead was a reliable tight end, Tim Wrightman was another sub in a starter's body. Wide receiver and world-class sprinter Willie Gault 'stretched' defenses with his speed and claimed he had worked in the offseason to improve his erratic pass routes. Flanker Dennis McKinnon, a third-year free agent from Florida State, had no fear of traffic and was one of Ditka's personal favorites.

Ditka and Ryan continued to clash over defensive philosophy. Ditka

1985 CHICAGO BEARS

Walter Payton, RB

Matt Suhey, FB

Calvin Thomas, FB

Dennis Gentry, RB

Thomas Sanders, RB

Ken Margerum, WR

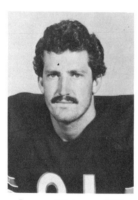
James Maness, WR

Brad Anderson, WR

Emery Moorehead, TE

Pat Dunsmore, TE

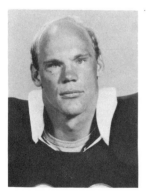
Mark Bortz, G

Stefan Humphries, G

Tom Thayer, G/C

Andy Frederick, T

Leslie Frazier, CB

preferred zone pass coverage. It allowed more yards, but caused more turnovers. Ryan's idea was to turn more people loose on the quarterback even if it meant occasionally counting on his cornerbacks in one-on-one coverage. If the pass rush was strong enough, said Ryan, the corners wouldn't be exposed long. And the pass rush was strong. Hampton constantly attracted two blockers inside. And as a result, right end Richard Dent led the NFC in sacks in 1984 with 17½.

Ryan's "46" defense, an ingenious concoction that featured two linebackers over the tight end, had been around for years and nobody had completely figured it yet. The "46" was where the Bears would miss Bell

Jim McMahon, QB

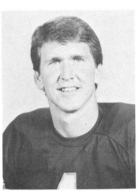
Steve Fuller, QB

Mike Tomczak, QB

Willie Gault, WR

Dennis McKinnon, WR

Tim Wrightman, TE

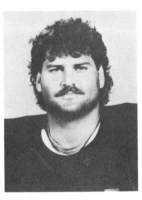
Jim Covert, T

Keith Van Horne, T

Jay Hilgenberg, C

Kurt Becker, G

Reggie Phillips, CB

Ken Taylor, CB

Kevin Butler, K

Maury Buford, P

Henry Waechter, DT

Mike Singletary, LB

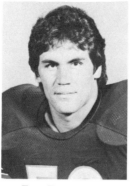

Ron Rivera, LB

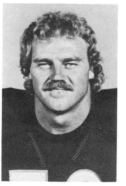

Cliff Thrift, LB

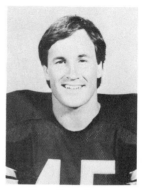

Dave Duerson, S

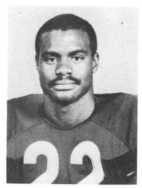

Gary Fencik, S

Shaun Gayle, S

Mike Richardson, CB

Mike Hartenstine, DE

Richard Dent, DE

Dan Hampton, DT

Steve McMichael, DT

Tyrone Keys, DE

William Perry, DT

Otis Wilson, LB

Wilber Marshall, LB

most. But Notre Dame strong safety Dave Duerson embarrassed nobody as a replacement. Ryan's free safety was Yale's Gary Fencik, who the homespun Ryan wryly referred to as "my resident genius."

The Bears' special teams took a giant step forward when Ditka and Tobin plucked Georgia's Kevin Butler on the fourth round. Veteran Bob Thomas had been a popular and reliable placekicker. But Butler simply had more foot. William Perry could have told them as much. He still remembered the 60-yarder Butler had kicked to beat Clemson the year before.

It was time for the real season to begin.

THE MAGICAL SEASON

William Perry was nothing more than an expensive and oversized bauble in the Bears' 38-28 season-opening victory over Tampa Bay at Soldier Field. Wearing a size-52 jersey, the largest on the team, and size-42 football pants, Perry watched McMahon lead the Bears back from a 21-7 deficit. The big play was a 29-yard interception return by cornerback Leslie Frazier that produced a touchdown on the second play of the second half.

"Perry's calves are so big," complained equipment manager Ray Earley, "that he can wear those white stretch socks just once. He stretches out the elastic so far that nobody can wear them again."

Defensive coordinator Ryan trusted Perry only in goal-line and short-yardage defenses. And for the second straight week the Bears didn't need him in any other capacity as they limited a good New England Patriot team to 116 yards on 56 plays in an impressive 20-7 victory.

But McMahon found himself in traction two days later suffering from spasms in his upper back. Later in the week an infection in his leg necessitated antibiotics. Steve Fuller started in his place before a Thursday night national television audience against the unbeaten Vikings in Minneapolis.

Trailing 17-9 with 7:22 remaining in the third quarter, Ditka finally relented to McMahon's sideline badgering, yanked Fuller and put him in the game. On his first play, McMahon dodged a Viking blitz, picked up a key block from Payton and found Willie Gault deep for a dramatic 70-yard touchdown. After a Wilber Marshall interception moments later McMahon

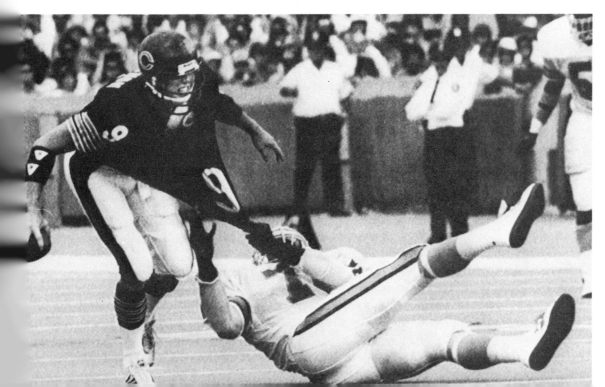

Tampa Bay's David Logan sacks Jim McMahon, but it matters little as the Bears open their 1985 season on September 8 with a 38-28 victory.

41

drilled Dennis McKinnon with a 25-yard touchdown pass on his next pass. Two plays. Two touchdowns.

The next time the Bears got the ball McMahon needed six plays to drive the Bears 68 yards, the score coming on a 43-yard bomb to McKinnon. In just six minutes and 40 seconds the Bears had scored 21 points. The final score: 33-24. "I can't explain what Jim sees or how he sees it," said an astonished Ditka after the game.

Three days later the Eagles upset the heavily-favored Washington Redskins, 19-6, at RFK Stadium. After the game Washington defensive end Dexter Manley launched a firestorm of controversy when asked about the Redskins' next opponent—the Bears. "We're gonna have to knock Walter Payton out of the game," said Manley. "I think McMahon's a little fragile. The guy can get hurt. But my main concern is Walter Payton. If we can get him, then we're gonna be all right."

Headlines begat headlines.

Manley apologized one week later after the Bears trounced the Redskins, 45-10, at Soldier Field. This time the Bears spotted their opponent a 10-0 lead. The visitors outgained the Bears 141 yards to two in the first quarter. The turnaround began when Willie Gault returned a kickoff 99 yards for a touchdown. Before the game was over McMahon had caught a touchdown pass from Walter Payton and Manley was a distant memory.

The night before the next game Ditka dined with personnel director Bill Tobin in Tampa. Both were increasingly frustrated with Ryan's refusal to play Perry on a more regular basis. The day after the draft Ditka had bumped into Tobin in the hallway of the Bears' Halas Hall headquarters. Perry was still fresh in both their minds. "Could you imagine," Ditka asked Tobin, "trying to tackle that guy?"

At the restaurant Tobin reminded Ditka of their conversation and said, "Why don't you put him in at fullback."

Ditka winked.

The next day the Bears won their fifth straight by the workmanlike score of 27-19. Perhaps they were looking ahead to their next opponent: the defending Super Bowl champion 49ers in San Francisco. Almost unnoticed, special teams coach Steve Kazor had inserted Perry onto his kickoff coverage teams.

Tobin arrived in the Bay Area early the following week to scout Stanford quarterback John Paye against UCLA the day before the 49ers' game. The Bears arrived later that Saturday. And when Ditka saw Tobin he pulled him aside. "Tobie," he said, "I put it in."

What he had "put in" was a straight-ahead running play with Perry carrying the ball. Ditka hadn't forgotten how 49er head coach Bill Walsh had utilized 264-pound guard Guy McIntyre as an "Angus" blocking back in San Francisco's 23-0 humiliation of the Bears in the previous year's NFC championship game.

Perry would be the payback. But first the Bears had to get into the position to use him. Ryan's defense took care of that. It limited the 49ers to 11 first downs and only 183 yards of total offense. Payton rushed for 83 yards in the second half alone.

On the Bears' last possession Ditka placed Perry in the backfield and one-upped Walsh by handing Perry the ball. Twice. He rumbled for two yards each time. The clock ran out and the Bears had upset the 49ers,

William Perry leaps to his feet after diving for a touchdown against Green Bay on October 21.

26-10. Perry's four-yard total was one more than the entire 49er offense rushed for in the second half.

Ditka insisted he wasn't trying to pay back anything. And even Walsh tried to downplay Perry's novel appearance. "I don't think," Walsh said of Perry, "he has a future as a running back."

The next day Ditka hinted otherwise. "You have to think about him on the goal line," said Ditka when asked if Perry would carry the ball again. It was remarkably clear thinking for a coach who had been arrested, handcuffed and booked for drunk driving the night before on his way home from the airport. The best was yet to come.

The Bears were now 6-0 and one of two remaining undefeated teams left in the NFL. The Rams, who would lose three of their next five, were the other. Appropriately, ABC-TV would beam the Bears' next game across the country on "Monday Night Football." The opponent: hated Green Bay.

"I never intended to make him a national hero," Ditka would say after the Bears' 23-7 victory over the Packers.

"Lightning struck," was the way Bear president Michael McCaskey put it.

For on October 21, 1985, the United States met "The Refrigerator."

Twice in the first half Ditka replaced Suhey with the 314-pound Perry near the goal line. And twice Perry delivered crushing blocks with textbook

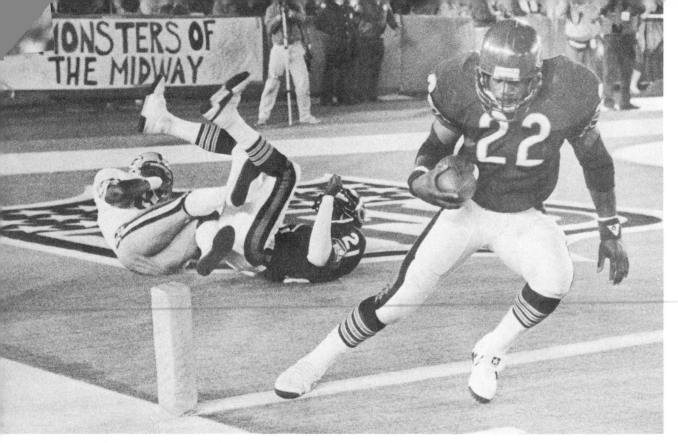

MONSTERS OF THE MIDWAY

Dave Duerson intercepts a Packer pass at the goal line in the 23-7 triumph.

technique on an unfortunate Packer linebacker named George Cumby. Both times Payton scored. In between, Perry dove over right guard for a touchdown of his own and celebrated with a thunderous spike in the end zone. ABC announcer O.J. Simpson said Perry looked like Marcus Allen.

"The first time I figured I'd take a side," said the 224-pound Cumby after the game. "It didn't matter which, I guess, because one is as big as another. The second time I hit him flush. That didn't work either." The third time? "I was outweighed by a few pounds."

The sportswriters had a field day. Wrote Chicago *Sun-Times* columnist Ray Sons: "What Mike Ditka did with William Perry last night was the best use of fat since bacon, the highest calling for a refrigerator since the first ice cube."

"I haven't seen a drive like that since *Rawhide,*" said Los Angeles *Times* columnist Mike Downey.

Chicago *Tribune* beat writer Don Pierson wrote about how the Bears had thrilled the nation with the "P" formation and the "single thing" backfield.

The Bears had started a trend.

For his part, Perry was unfazed. "No style," he said when specifically asked to describe his running style. "After I get the ball in the open field, I just go straight ahead." After seven games Perry trailed Payton, the NFL's all-time leading rusher, by only 13,828 yards.

And the rest of the country was about to find out what Perry's teammates already knew: William Perry wasn't a wordsmith but he knew how to make a statement about himself. And it was always a cheerful one. He couldn't walk across the Bear locker room without being affectionately pelted with rolled-up sweatsocks or jockstraps. To the rest of the Bears he was simply, "Fridge." Soon, the fans picked up on it. "Fridge Fever" broke out.

44

"Maybe President Reagan could use Perry as a bargaining chip at Geneva promising to have Ditka mothball his refrigerator in return for Russian willingness to abandon production of a new MIG," wrote Sons.

"Manute Bol (the 7-7 NBA center) and William Perry could go to a Halloween party dressed as the No. 10," said Downey.

Even the Washington *Post* got into the act. "Stop That Refrigerator," an editorial proclaimed three days after Perry's touchdown. "In a nationally-televised game Monday night, the Bears wheeled out their giant, whose true vocation is supposed to be defensive lineman and pressed him into service as a running back, as in, 'Is your refrigerator running?'" read the *Post* editorial. "On a play at the goal line, they got him balanced, put the ball in his vegetable crisper and sort of toppled William Perry onto a group of terrified Green Bay Packers."

"Perry," concluded the newspaper that chased Richard Nixon from the Presidency, "is a prominent example of someone who is having his cake and eating it, too, and, to all of us who are trying to lose some weight, he is a beacon of hope—one that shines only when you open the door."

Sports Illustrated followed up with a full-length feature that detailed Perry's midweek visits to a local health club where he played basketball in order to shed pounds for his biweekly weigh-ins. SI also quoted McCaskey, an Ivy Leaguer from Yale, as saying, "Pro football is one of the last refuges in America for eccentrics."

Penn State coach Joe Paterno had watched Perry's blocks against the

Walter Payton eludes Minnesota's Rufus Bess for a touchdown as he leads the Bears to a 27-9 decision on October 27.

Packers and was impressed more with Perry's technique than his size. "He'd be a force even if he weighed 200 pounds," Paterno said.

Prior to Game Eight, a rematch with the Vikings at Soldier Field, Perry was the public focal point. The New York Giants' rotund general manager, George Young, called Perry a "designated rhino." But he meant it as a compliment. "Just because the guy is big and fat doesn't mean he can't catch and throw," said Young. "Offensive linemen used to fascinate me because some of them could catch a ball better than a running back."

Viking offensive coordinator Jerry Burns threatened to stack 185-pound running back Darrin Nelson on top of 318-pound offensive lineman Curtis (Boo-Boo) Rouse in what he called "our piggyback formation." Ditka mumbled something about responding with 5-8 running back Dennis Gentry in the "old elephant and mouse trick." Imaginations ran wild.

"It's every man's dream," said 302-pound rookie Viking nose man Tim (Icebox) Newton. "My running style would be like Walter Payton's style, quick and elusive. A lot of moves and a lot of power." Newton and Perry had been roommates at the January scouting combine when Perry had pegged the scale at more than 350 pounds. "William was always complaining about the food," said Newton of Perry. "But that never stopped him from eating it."

Meanwhile the Bears' offense led the league in scoring. And a Pro Football Writers' poll was unanimous in its selection of the Bears as the NFL's No. 1 team. When somebody asked Ditka when he planned to use Perry at quarterback, he said, "as soon as he jumps over the goalpost."

Reaction among the league's other coaches was mixed. "What are you going to say if he fumbles because he's only practiced the play four times?" warned Seattle coach Chuck Knox. "It's the greatest thing in the world when you win. When you lose, everything you do looks stupid."

"An interesting concept," said Cardinal coach Jim Hanifan of Perry. "Hell, if you can get a 300-pounder who's got that kind of explosiveness, I'd say that's pretty damn good coaching."

How explosive was Perry? "Between the hips and the knees, he may be the strongest that's ever played the game," said Bill Tobin.

"Maybe that's where we're moving in football," said Washington coach Joe Gibbs. "That could be the next evolution."

"There is no defensive player in his right mind who would tackle William Perry," said Raider cornerback Lester Hayes. Added Viking linebacker Dennis Johnson: "When you go in, you have to carry an elephant gun with you. That guy is like a Mack truck going downhill."

"I don't know who would want to face that guy," said St. Louis personnel director Larry Wilson, a former All-Pro defensive back. "If he came at me trying to throw a block, I'd probably run away."

Apparently the only thing that frightened Perry was becoming obese. "He's always making comments about fat guys," said Tyrone Keys. "During a game he'll yell, 'Look at that fat guy over there.'"

But against the Vikings Perry didn't run, throw, catch or jump over the goalpost. There simply weren't any appropriate goal-line situations. He did, however, make his first NFL quarterback sack, nailing Minnesota's Tommy Kramer. "I came here to sack quarterbacks, not to score touchdowns," insisted the Fridge. It was the first game Ryan used him on passing downs. "That's what we drafted him for," said Ditka.

"I just swimmed over him," said Perry describing the move suggested by teammate Steve McMichael that helped him beat Viking center Dennis Swilley. "They tried to block him one-on-one," said McMichael. "You can't do that."

The Bears were nursing a tenuous 13-7 lead early in the third period when linebacker Otis Wilson intercepted a Kramer pass and returned it 23 yards for a touchdown. Later the Vikings drove to the Bear one. But on second-and-goal linebacker Wilber Marshall cut in front of Darrin Nelson and intercepted Kramer again.

"That was the key play," said Viking tight end Steve Jordan. "We had the momentum at that point. But that got them and the crowd pumped up."

Kramer, who had thrown for 436 yards against the Bears in Minneapolis, completed only 16 passes for 176 yards. Payton, meanwhile, gained 118 yards in the 27-9 decision. It was his third straight 100-yard game. "Payton seems to be as good as ever," said Bud Grant. "He certainly has been a credit to the game. I just wish he wouldn't be so creditable to us."

In Anaheim that same day, the 49ers breezed past the Rams, 28-14. The Bears were the only remaining unbeaten team in the NFL. And suddenly Perry was a starter.

That was the announcement out of Bear camp before Game Nine, a rematch against the Packers in Green Bay. Hampton would move from right tackle to left end, a position that enabled him to protect his surgical knees

Dan Hampton leaps over downed Viking to corner quarterback Tommy Kramer.

from double-team blocks. Perry took Hampton's spot inside. Ditka said it was his idea. Ryan claimed he made the move because 32-year-old left end Mike Hartenstine was showing his age.

The Packers were still smarting from the humiliation of losing at Soldier Field two weeks earlier. They felt Ditka had rubbed Perry in their noses. Fights broke out early and often. Officials ejected Packer cornerback Mark Lee when he rode Payton out of bounds and over the Bear bench. They didn't eject Green Bay defensive back Ken Stills when he leveled Matt Suhey several seconds after the whistle had blown.

"It was a very physical game," understated Green Bay coach Forrest Gregg afterward. And the Bears won, 16-10, in large part because of a four-yard pass from McMahon to Perry. Oh yes, Payton rushed for 192 yards.

On Perry's touchdown he lined up as a wingback left. When he went in motion to the right, the Packers braced themselves for a Payton rush behind Perry. Cumby charged toward Perry, who elegantly sidestepped him and waltzed into the end zone, where he calmly grabbed McMahon's soft toss. "It was the first pass that I have ever caught in any game," said Perry.

And it sparked another hysterical round of Perrymania. For the next several days sportscasters around the country showed Perry's touchdown forward, backward and in slow motion. One songwriter rewrote the old Gerry and the Pacemakers' tune of the '60s, changing the title from "Ferry Crossed The Mersey" to "Perry Crossed My Jersey."

Even Gregg was amused. "He was beautiful, wasn't he?" said the Packer coach when asked about Perry's touchdown. "He's a heck of an

William Perry catches a pass from Jim McMahon for a touchdown against Green Bay on November 3.

The media descends on the jubilant, pass-receiving Perry after the Bears made it nine in a row against Green Bay.

athlete. You watch him on kickoffs. He gets down the field. You have to be darned impressed by a guy like him."

"We just saw this big guy waddling around back there," said Green Bay linebacker Brian Noble. "How he got around us, I don't know. The next thing I know he's rolling into the end zone." Cumby didn't think it was as funny this time. He was unavailable for comment.

"How can you practice against a 300-pound guy coming out of the backfield?" Noble demanded to know. "You practice for that pattern to be run by a normal fullback. You try to expect anything, but we weren't expecting a 300-pound something-or-other to run a pass pattern. How is he going to outrun anybody? The coverage was blown, that was it."

Suddenly Perry was the hottest commercial property this side of "Miami Vice." Like Glenn Campbell's *Rhinestone Cowboy* he was getting cards and letters from people he didn't even know. And offers coming over the phone. To be sure, Perry's presence served to keep the Bears loose. But at least one observer suggested he was unfairly diverting attention away from people like Payton.

"In a sense, it's a travesty," agreed Hampton, "because Walter's the greatest player ever and William's more or less an oddity." But, Hampton added, "I don't think you can have enough of William because there's so much of him to go around. He's a 300-pound good guy and I'm proud of him."

49

All-Pro Raider defensive lineman Howie Long predicted Perry wouldn't last. "When he plays eight or nine straight games at noseguard he won't be running the ball too much or running a fly pattern," said Long.

"I never argue with anybody as smart as Howie Long," answered Ditka. "Or is it Huey Long?"

"If they asked me to play offense, I'd do it," said Howie Long. "But I don't have any desire to do it."

Long admitted he admired Perry. "The guy's becoming a folk hero," he said. "I think it's a riot. The guy doesn't look a pound under 350." Perry claimed his weight had dropped to 308. Ditka said 311. The Bear press guide said 318. The team's weekly press release said 325.

Jim Murray, the longtime Los Angeles *Times* sports columnist, analyzed Perry this way: "I don't know about you, but every street game we ever played in, if a guy 100 pounds bigger than the rest showed up, there was no one to tell him he was going to play in the obscurity of defense or the sacrificial slot of blocking. He wanted the ball and he got the ball. If you were smart, you said to your teammates, 'OK, you get the big guy. I'll fade back in case he passes.'"

On the Wednesday before the Bears would run their record to 10-0 with a 24-3 victory over the Lions at Soldier Field, McMahon came up with a sore throwing shoulder. By Friday it was obvious he wouldn't play against Detroit. Ditka was upset because he hadn't been informed when the injury occurred three weeks earlier. McMahon was upset because he had been a fast healer all his life and the shoulder was getting worse instead of better. Suspiciously inaccessible Bear physician Clarence Fossier diagnosed the injury as a bruise of the acrimioclavicular joint. After a subsequent examination of McMahon and a conferral with Northwestern Memorial Hospital's Dr. Michael Schaefer, Fossier decided McMahon had tendinitis. He prescribed rest and medication.

Fuller's first start of the year was made easier by Payton and Suhey. The Bears called 21 running plays against the league's worst-rated rushing defense before throwing their first pass. Payton finished with 107 yards, Suhey got 102. Fuller threw only 13 passes but gained valuable confidence. "I felt like there had been some doubt whether we could win without Jim," he said. "The idea we'd fall flat on our faces and not be able to do anything without Jim discouraged me a little bit. But the guys rallied around me and we did all right." The defense allowed 106 yards. Perry had two more sacks but didn't carry the ball in the three offensive plays Ditka used him.

The Bears were now only the 12th team in NFL history to win their first 10 games. Playoff talk surfaced. The NFC Central division title was a foregone conclusion. So Hampton talked about the importance of earning the home-field advantage throughout the playoffs. "I'd be miserable playing here in January," he said. "But I'd much rather be miserable here than go out and get beat in Los Angeles. Then I'd really be miserable."

By now Perry had already appeared on the "CBS Morning News" and NBC's "Today" show. But both programs had sent camera crews to Chicago. They bearded him in his own den. The day after the Lion game Perry, his wife and personal manager Conrad Ford flew to New York for a taping of NBC's "Late Night with David Letterman." A Chicago *Tribune* reporter accompanied Perry on the plane. A Chicago *Sun-Times* reporter met him at LaGuardia. Also waiting at the gate were crews from two local television stations and a reporter for the New York *Post*.

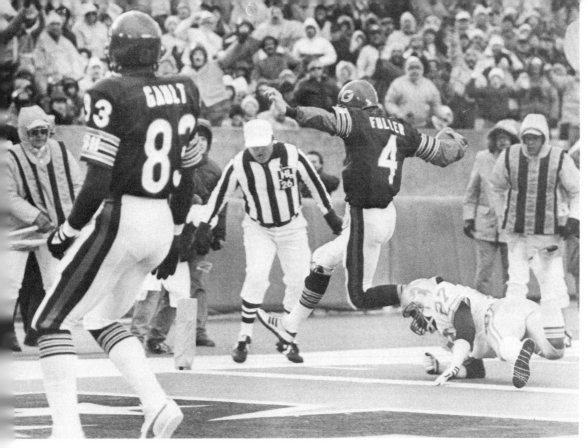

Quarterback Steve Fuller, replacing the injured Jim McMahon, makes his first start a winning one as the unbeaten Bears rack up their 10th straight against the Lions, 24-3, on November 10.

"Watch out New York," warned the female reporter from WABC-TV as the cameras whirred. "The Refrigerator has landed." Finally, the driver from the Letterman show pried Perry away from an adoring mob and whisked him off to the waiting limo. Once inside, the driver reached over to the passenger side of the Volvo Stretch GLE, opened the glove compartment and adjusted the electric air-shock absorbers. Perry settled comfortably in the back seat. In less than two hours Perry would be swapping bon mots with the same talk-show host who once called overweight Atlanta pitcher Terry Forster "a fat tub of goo."

"I understand in Japan people actually worship you," Letterman would say. The audience would laugh. "I've heard that before," Perry would reply.

But right now the limo was hustling across the Triboro Bridge, down FDR Drive and up to the front door of "Thirty Rock"—NBC's Manhattan headquarters. It was rush hour. "New York," said a wide-eyed Perry peering out at the city lights. "Look at this place."

In the hallway outside the studio Perry caused the same furor he had inspired at the airport. Assistant producers, pages, cameramen and even members of Paul Shaffer's ultra-cool band stopped and stared. "Tom Selleck just sort of walked in and walked out when he was here," said Letterman aide Laurie Guthrie. "It was nothing like this."

A half hour before showtime Letterman strolled down the hall wearing a Walter Payton jersey bearing the number 34. Thirty minutes later he burst onto the set wearing a coat and tie. Perry's people had privately feared Letterman might savage Perry on the air. But the wildly enthusiastic response that met Perry's introduction cautioned Letterman. "I heard he might tell some hard jokes on me," Perry said later. "But there were no surprises at all. He was a nice guy."

Among other things, Perry told Letterman he eats just one meal a day. (Letterman: "You're going to waste away to nothing.") Perry also said he wouldn't mind returning kickoffs and that he throws "just like Roger Staubach." Finally Letterman got Perry to admit to having consumed 48 beers following a college victory over North Carolina. "It was a big game," said Perry. Letterman showed a tape of Perry running for his touchdown in the first Green Bay game. Then he showed a tape of Perry catching the touchdown pass in the second Green Bay game. Damned if Perry didn't catch the ball again on the replay.

The Letterman people wanted to do a bit with Perry carrying tiny child star Emmanuel Lewis of TV's "Webster" on his shoulders. But the boss of the 43-inch Lewis' entourage refused. Perry had brought along a deflated football to present to Letterman on the air. The pigskin had been gutted and filled with a slab of ribs. But the Letterman people said no props. Through it all Perry didn't flinch. By controlling his nerves he also controlled his most distracting speech habit. "He only said 'you know' twice," said Clemson sports information's Tim Bourret proudly. Bourret watched Perry's performance in South Carolina.

Suddenly the show was over. Back in the hallway *People* Magazine waited along with more reporters and an army of photographers. More Fridge Fever. More snapshots. More interviews. By now Letterman's security people had learned of another mob waiting in the lower lobby. So they commandeered a service elevator and spirited Perry out a side door and into a different limo. Still, people were there grabbing, shouting, screaming and pushing pens in his face.

Finally, the driver orchestrated Perry's escape from New York. And while personal manager Ford sat up front riding shotgun and Sherry, pregnant with the Perrys' second child, curled up for a quick nap in the back, the Refrigerator contemplated the magnitude of what was happening to him. He was quiet and relaxed—the eye in the center of the storm. Media prophet Marshall McLuhan would have been jealous of his analysis. "I just take the publicity and go," Perry said. "I don't live off it. Some people take it and live off it. And they'll run it into the ground. They'll run it into other players' faces. That's not me.

"I just take it one day and let it go the next day. I had it all through college and it was wonderful then. Me and my wife and my little girl, we loved it. It was fun. But now all it is is crazy. It's wild. You couldn't even have dreamed this much. Nothing can remain this intense, though. It's like Michael Jackson came out with all those records. They didn't stay up but for so long. Everybody knows of him now. And when he appears somewhere they would like to see him. It might be something like that with me. But as far as me taking it and running with it . . . no, I don't think that'll happen. I'll just let it go.

"What goes up must come back down. And everything will come back to reality. And I'll be still just like I am right now. I haven't changed a bit since Day One."

On December 17 Perry was scheduled to make this same, long, strange, one-day trip for an appearance on the "Tonight Show" with Johnny

Perry goes one-on-one with the show's host on "Late Night with David Letterman."

Carson. But his next challenge was the 7-3 Dallas Cowboys in Texas Sunday on national TV.

The pregame buildup centered around three things: Ditka's relationship with Landry; the nasty nature of the Cowboys' 15-13 win over the Bears in the preseason and McMahon's worsening shoulder condition. Ditka downplayed the first, the players downplayed the second, but the media couldn't ignore the third. McMahon didn't practice all week. But the Bears didn't make McMahon's status official until Friday when they downgraded him from questionable to doubtful on the injury report. He would not play. Fuller would start. "I will just try to avoid the big mistake," Fuller said.

And he did. Cowboy quarterbacks Danny White and Gary Hogeboom should have been so lucky. With less than two minutes remaining in the first period Maury Buford's coffin corner punt backed the Cowboys up to their own two. On first down Hampton, who had beaten right tackle Jim Cooper with a vicious arm-whip maneuver, batted a White pass into the air. The 6-5 Dent alertly plucked the ball from the sky and negotiated one yard for a touchdown. The Bears led, 7-0.

Five and a half minutes into the second period the Bears' lead was 10-0

53

when left linebacker Otis Wilson shot clear on a blitz and hammered White unconscious. All season, Wilson's announced individual goal was a berth on the NFC Pro Bowl squad. "If I don't make that thing now," he said after the game, "Stevie Wonder must be counting the votes."

Hogeboom replaced White. And less than four minutes later it was 17-0 when cornerback Mike Richardson picked off a hurried pass and waltzed 36 yards for six points. Once again it was Wilson who forced the bad throw. On the Bears' next possession Ditka inserted Perry on first-and-goal from the Cowboy two. Fridge probed right tackle for one yard but didn't break the plane of the end zone. Fuller dove over on the next play to make it 24-0. The rout was on.

The eventual 44-0 embarassment the Bears inflicted on the Cowboys was the worst loss in the history of the Dallas franchise. Payton ran for 132 yards, his sixth-straight 100-yard game. The defense allowed only 171 yards to an offense that entered the game tied for second in NFL total offense. And the Bears clinched the NFC Central division crown for the second straight year. It was the earliest division-clinching since the league switched to a 16-game regular season in 1978. "I don't think I could have dreamed it any better," said McMichael. "A good old-fashioned country licking," Landry called it.

Clarvoyant cartoonist Jeff MacNelly, a Pulitzer Prize winner, called a pass play for William Perry the week before Perry caught one for a touchdown against Green Bay.

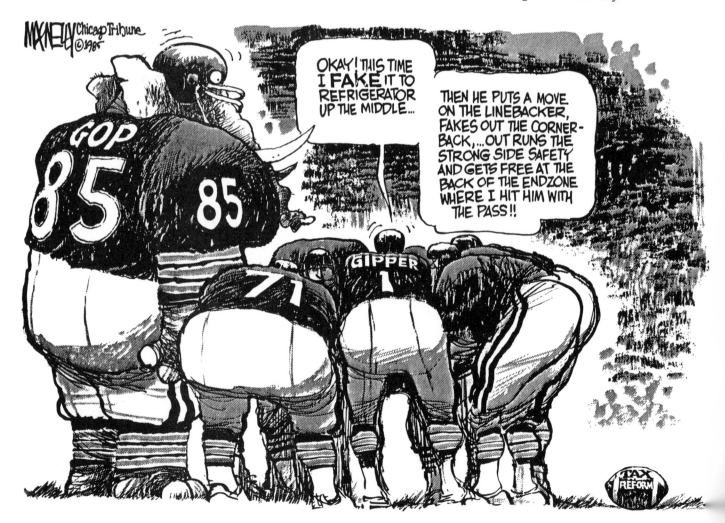

After the game Singletary lingered on the field briefly, looking up into the rapidly emptying stands. "I want witnesses," he shouted. "I want witnesses."

Perry disappointed no one late in the third period when Ditka trotted him out in yet another goal-line situation. Bored with their team's 24-0 deficit, the home crowd cheered lustily when Perry shambled onto the field. On third-and-goal from the Cowboy two, Perry was uproariously guilty of illegal use of the hands. The Refrigerator had buried the first defender to get in his way. But when the rest of the Cowboys stacked Payton up at the one, Perry scrambled to his feet and took matters into his own massive hands by hoisting Payton and attempting to throw him over the goal line.

"I was trying to pull some of those people off him," the Fridge pleaded after the game. "When I got to Walter, I wanted to help him, too." When Perry got back to the sidelines, his teammates explained the problem. "They told me I couldn't do that," he said. The penalty pushed the Bears back to the 12-yard line. And they eventually had to settle for a Kevin Butler field goal.

"I'm sure I've been carried into the end zone before," said Payton. "But never by anyone of Perry's stature. I didn't even know it was him. He said he was kind of trying to keep the defensive players off of me. I appreciate that."

"I guess William just figures he can carry the ball or the ballcarrier into the end zone," said center Jay Hilgenberg.

"It shows the determination he has," said Ditka.

The Bears were now 11-0. At Aiken High School, Perry's teams finished 33-10. Clemson's Tigers were 37-6-2 in his four years. All of which made Perry 81-16-2 in nine years of organized football. That's a remarkable winning percentage of .835.

After the game, the usual army of reporters gathered around Perry's locker, unconcerned that he had only made one tackle. "I'm just having fun," he said, reiterating the stock line that summed up his reaction to the bizarre chain of events that had transformed him from a struggling rookie into a national celebrity.

Meanwhile the Bears were already looking for a warm-weather site to practice for their early January playoff opener. Winter was coming. Soon Chicago would be an outdoor refrigerator.

The ultimate goal, of course, was New Orleans, site of Super Bowl XX on January 26, 1986.

The making of a Big Mac commercial: Perry awaits his cue as teammates Dave Duer-son (left) Steve McMichael (rear right) and Dan Hampton put on the feed bag.

THE SELLING OF A REFRIGERATOR

The day after the Dallas slaughter on November 17, *Newsweek* began finalizing plans for a story featuring the Bears. The three principals they planned to focus on were Ditka, Payton and Perry. Meanwhile *Sports Illustrated*'s editors decided to make the Bears their cover story subject for the second time in less than six weeks.

The next afternoon newspaper offices around the Chicago area began receiving press releases announcing: "Montgomery Ward Joins William Perry To Launch 'Fridge Fever'!"

"Montgomery Ward," read the blurb, "has joined with the Bears' William 'The Refrigerator' Perry to unleash 'Fridge Fever' Thursday, November 21 at the new Montgomery Ward store in St. Charles. The rookie sensation will debut his new Fridge Fever hat, which will go on sale Thursday at the store. Perry will appear from 6 P.M. to 8 P.M. Thursday in [where else?] the Appliance Center, one of the new specialty stores created by Montgomery Ward. He will give away autographed pictures to the first 2,000 customers at the store.

"He will also unveil Fridge Fever, the new rallying cry created by Perry and his management consultants, Bry and Associates, St. Louis. 'Fridge Fever is exactly what has been happening, not only in Chicago, but all across the country, since William scored his first touchdown on Monday Night Football,' said agent Jim Steiner. 'He's becoming a legend with football fans everywhere.'"

"We are excited and proud to associate our name with William Perry," said Ward's official Melba Graffius. "Just as our new advertising slogan 'Things Are Changing' represents a new direction for Montgomery Ward, The Refrigerator is changing the image of the Chicago Bears."

Fridge Fever hats cost $7.

That same day Perry filmed a commercial for McDonald's. Coca Cola and Pontiac were at the head of the waiting list. The selling of William Perry had begun in earnest.

Weeks earlier Bry and Associates, which represents more than 100 professional athletes including Darryl Strawberry, Rickey Henderson, Dan Hampton and Steve McMichael, had assigned three people from its football division to handle Perry's account full time. The three barely had enough time to sift through all the offers much less pause to consider the sociological phenomenon they were representing. But plenty of other people had theories about how an overweight rookie from the rural south had turned into a national celebrity overnight.

"The guy is a folk hero," said Joe Brouillard, a retired image maker for

57

the J. Walter Thompson ad firm. "To me, it's a positive thing. Here's a guy who came out of nowhere, an apparently pretty good athlete. I commend the coach for what he's doing with him."

On the day of the Cowboy game the Dallas *Morning News* ran a story on page one in which writer Dan Barreiro referred to Perry as a person "who never met a manwich he didn't like."

"Perry has arrived," wrote Barreiro, "not just in the Dallas area . . . The Fridge has arrived in Chicago, too. And New York, Boston and San Francisco. And Paducah, Poughkeepsie and Kokomo. And any other city, town or village in which at least one man, woman or child CAN pinch an inch. Yes, fat is truly a universal language."

If this was the "me" generation, Perry represented all of me. "This country is terribly weight-conscious," said New York political consultant David Garth. "We're embarrassed by our weight which is why we're always dieting, running and jogging, trying to lose weight. Through a guy like the Refrigerator, we can fantasize what we would do in our fat bodies."

"What people don't understand is not just any 300-pound guy can do it," said teammate McMichael of Perry's on-the-field accomplishments. "Some of the other big guys who played in this league were slobs. William is a very good athlete." And he was showing other big and tall men across the country there was hope.

Perry's college defensive coordinator insisted there was too much emphasis on Perry's weight which, incidentally, had dropped to 302 after the Dallas win. "I think P [Perry] could weigh 500 pounds and play like an ordinary guy," Clemson's Tom Harper said. "Have you ever really LOOKED at him? Have you ever seen an upper profile like that? I'd see his huge shadow in the film room sometimes and I'd think I was looking at a Kodiak bear."

Part of the reason for Perry's weight problem, Harper said, was his good nature. "After games at Clemson on Saturday afternoon he'd take his wife, Sherry, down to a local pizza place and everybody wanted to buy him a pizza. Well, being the kind of person he is, if you're nice enough to buy a pizza, he'll eat it. Even if he's full."

None other than George Plimpton, the professional amateur, cited Perry's nickname as a key to his popularity and marketability. "If Perry was called 'Tubs' he wouldn't have the appeal," said the droll Plimpton. "I think the fans adore this sort of thing. There is always a call for a freak or a seven-foot basketball center in sports. The oddities—they are held with great affection. In the long run fans would rather see Walter Payton run 40 yards than Perry go for one or two. As a pure athlete, Perry's not there yet."

Then there was the "comic relief" hypothesis. The William Perry of Shakespeare's day was a splay-toed, ale-bellied loveable old debaucher named Jack Falstaff. While Falstaff entertained the groundlings with pie-in-the-face humor, Shakespeare's other characters went about the serious business of life, death, love, hate, peace and war.

While the Bears were going about the business of remaining undefeated, Perry entertained teammates, fans and the critics, all of whom might otherwise have been dwelling on the pressures of being unbeaten if Perry wasn't around to unburden their minds.

"It's almost like winning the lottery," said Ditka of the Perry phenomenon after the first Green Bay game.

"Falstaff sweats to death and lards the earth as he walks along," wrote

Shakespeare in *King Henry IV*. Perry sweated a lot, too. But he could also play a little. Falstaff could not.

CBS-TV, the network of the National Football Conference, immediately knew what it had in Perry. "For sheer promotional value with pure fun attached, there has never been anything to compare—output to amount of publicity—in three decades of the NFL's prominence on television," wrote TV critic Jack Craig in *The Sporting News*.

"If the public didn't take to him, television focus wouldn't have meant much," said Val Pinchbeck, television coordinator for the NFL. CBS even arranged for John Madden and George Allen to debate on the air whether Perry was a trend. Madden said he was, the stodgy Allen said he wasn't.

During the week leading up to the first Bears-Lions game CBS increased the coverage of its telecast from 11 percent of the country to 50 percent. Was it the Perry factor? "Let's say the Refrigerator is hot," said CBS official Susan Kerr oxymoronically.

"The one thing certain about television and William Perry," concluded Craig, "is that he is providing a lot of fun. That has always been in short supply in the NFL, one more reason for the popularity of the Refrigerator."

"Football is deadly, deadly predictable," said Bruce Ogilvie, a San Jose State psychologist. Ogilvie said Perry gave football "an element of lovely fantasy, an escapism for most fans. There is a phenomenon around which one can fantasize about the possible."

Social-minded *New York Times* sports columnist George Vecsey planted his tongue firmly in his cheek and called the Perry phenomenon a "dangerous" turn of events. Vecsey said San Francisco's Bill Walsh was an innovator when he used Guy McIntyre in the Angus formation. But Vecsey added if Walsh had given McIntyre the ball, that would have made him a "Bolshevik." Ditka, on the other hand, was different. "Mike Ditka's strain of rebellion stems from his playing at Pitt in that brief window of renaissance man from 1958-60 when college football had a limited substitution rule," wrote Vecsey. "Ditka played defensive end, linebacker, receiver and punter, and, like the Manchurian Candidate, had the seeds of anarchy planted deep in his psyche."

"We owe him [Ditka] a piece of the action, don't we?" asked agent Steiner. Then he started moving off to another appointment with another potential client. "We started out with a guy who, in the view of others, was the rock bottom pick of the first round," Steiner added. "Now, he's the hottest property in football, maybe in all of sports. It's a delicate situation. We feel we have to be careful on William's behalf, because it spirals to the Chicago Bears. They are a team, and we don't want the team to develop any bad feelings. We want to work with the Bears and create the type of image that is right for him and select the opportunities that benefit him and the other people he's associated with.

"I think you can make a strong argument that no other athlete has ever had the siege that has come upon William Perry in such a short time. It's fabulous for William. I imagine some people would cut off an arm for this kind of attention. In the beginning we were getting maybe 10 or 12 calls an hour. It's way beyond that now. The opportunities for him are astonishing.

"A number of things have contributed to it. First, it's the way he came into the league, heavily criticized. There was the weight issue. The way Ditka used him in the San Francisco game was thought of as a retaliatory measure and then all of a sudden he played a key role in the Monday Night Game. That got him national exposure. He was 'The Refrigerator,' not a wasted draft choice. It was the element of surprise."

By the first Detroit game Steiner reported endorsement requests had grown to 30 a day. So he polished his pitch. "The thing that makes great athletes is the fact that they've got ice water in their veins," Steiner said. "William's got ice water running through his body."

And maybe a little cholesterol? "That's true," Steiner conceded. "There may be a little sugar water in there."

The Bear public relations staff, which coordinated Perry's appearances locally, hired an extra assistant to handle the Perry crunch that was accompanying the general interest in the undefeated Bears. It started to get bad the day after the Green Bay Monday Night Game.

Media assistant Bryan Harlan got a letter from a group of lawyers and judges from Syracuse, New York, who had formed a fan club. They wanted pictures of Perry. Said the letter: "The day after the Green Bay-Chicago game we decided that the Fridge definitely deserved a fan club as he represents a new breed of running backs, that is the high-bloat, short-yardage, limited-porpoise back. We have decided to call the fan club 'The Central New York Frigidaires.' We plan to hold meetings the day after every opportunity he gets to play offense."

A fan club in Chicago offered free membership to anyone weighing more than 300 pounds. By late November it had gained eight such members.

Harlan escorted Perry to a public appearance at Shenannigan's, a fast-lane singles bar on Chicago's swinging Division Street. Shenannigan's regularly pays two Bear players to mingle with patrons and sign autographs after home games. "I booked Fridge before he became famous," said Harlan. "And normally on Sunday afternoons there's no line outside. But for Perry they had to put up wooden horses to keep people away from him while he signed autographs. The people were chanting, 'Perry, Perry.'"All three local network affiliates sent camera crews.

The normal $300 appearance fee for rookies was unworkable for Perry because of the incredible demand. So the Bears turned the requests over to Steiner, who immediately jacked the fee up to $3,500 hoping to discourage the volume. "That didn't help," said Harlan. So they moved the asking price up to $5,000. There were still plenty of takers.

The most bizarre request came from *Omni* magazine. *Omni* decided to solicit celebrities for their opinion on the theory of male pregnancy. "Enough is enough," Harlan told the magazine. "I've got to draw the line somewhere."

Together, Steiner, Harlan and Ken Valdiserri, his immediate supervisor, fought to keep Fridge Fever from becoming a sideshow and, worse, a distraction to Perry and his teammates. Their goal: sanity. "I think we can handle it the proper way by only associating William with quality companies and long-term relationships," Steiner said.

So when the guy called wanting to promote a William Perry 360-degree slam dunk show with 5-7 NBA mighty mite Spud Webb, Steiner politely declined. He did the same when another huckster in Kentucky wanted Perry to wrestle a real bear.

Conrad Ford, Steiner's associate, had met Perry at the Walter Camp

Foundation following Perry's senior season. They developed a relationship that led to Perry's signing with Bry and Associates. "Usually our standard line to a player is that we'll handle his business affairs and promotional affairs as and if they come about," Steiner said. "No one knew the 'as and if' would be this intense."

Steiner figured Perry would make more than $100,000 in endorsements in 1985 without even trying. He didn't rule out the possibility of Perry eventually earning $1,000,000 off the field. "It's not going to happen in the next six months," he said. "But it could. It depends upon what happens with the Bears. It depends upon whether he stays healthy and plays and if they continue to use him as an offensive player."

Not only had songwriters written a passel of original lyrics extolling Perry, but disc jockeys had dubbed Perry lines into old standards like "Locomotion" by Little Eva and "Revolution" by the late John Lennon. After the Dallas game it was hard to turn on the radio without hearing one of them every 15 minutes. Even the *Wall Street Journal* featured Perry. The Chicago *Sun-Times* published a full-page color poster of Perry.

Meanwhile, Steiner arranged for Perry to take communications lessons from a company that called itself Communispond. Communispond encouraged Perry to relax in front of the camera and remember humorous stories that could be easily repeated. It worked.

The pitchmen had calculated the public would want products like Refrigerator T-shirts, Refrigerator salad bars, Refrigerator bathroom scales, Refrigerator Quarter Pounders, Refrigerator Diet Coke, Refrigerator haircare products, Refrigerator toy robots, Refrigerator low-fat cheese, Refrigerator refrigerator movers, Refrigerator refrigerators and many, many, many, many more.

Coca-Cola selected Perry and McMahon for a commercial scheduled to begin airing in December. At the taping of Perry's first McDonald's commercial, Hampton complained, "I'm just an extra." Steve McMichael and safety Dave Duerson rounded out the cast. The joke in the commercial was that Perry surprised the person behind the counter by ordering a Diet Coke. But he also ordered four McD.L.T.s and two large orders of fries.

Old habits died hard.

CHAPTER EIGHT

ALL IN THE FAMILY

By midseason the young Perry family finally graduated from the drab existence of hotel living and moved into a house in suburban Mundelein. Mundelein is a small, mostly white, northwest suburb of Chicago, minutes from the Bears' Lake Forest practice facility. A local paper ran an editorial welcoming the young couple and its daughter to their community. "That made me feel great," said Perry.

And, said Perry, he would feel even better when the drapes arrived, the wallpaper man finished and the deck got completed. Meanwhile three-year-old Latavia Shenique Perry was still adjusting to her daddy's new status. "Every time she's there when he's signing autographs she gets a little jealous," said Sherry Perry. "She gets a little pad out and starts scribbling and handing that out. And at games on Sundays she wants to go down onto the field."

But Latavia's biggest adjustment was getting used to her father's new number—72. At Clemson he wore 66.

From the beginning, William loved Latavia Shenique in the best tradition of daddies and daughters. "I've never seen a man take up so much time with a child," said Sherry. "He loves to get her all fixed up with a pretty new dress and ribbons in her hair and take his little girl for a walk.

"He just loves to show her off. From the time she was born, though, he's been buying her little boy toys. I have to keep reminding him that she's a little girl." At Clemson William bought Latavia a battery-operated truck. "She rode around in it, and spent most of the time chasing William or me around in the backyard." said Sherry.

The only record of Perry ever having anything close to a mean streak was a brief period during high school. Sherry quickly set him straight. She decided Perry and his friends were bullying people, making jokes at their expense. She dumped him for a year. "William was real loud, very demanding and pushy," Sherry recalled. "He would pick people up and swing them around. Then he kind of changed. He got more mature and started taking things serious."

"I had to mature," said Perry. "I thought I was going to lose Sherry. I stopped joking around." But he did have one last laugh during his senior year in high school when he picked Sherry up and stuffed her into a garbage can. "She laughed," said Perry. "And I laughed."

"I didn't have any choice," said Sherry.

Sherry still cringes when her husband roughhouses with their daughter. "He plays with Tay Tay so rough I sometimes think he's going to kill her," said Sherry. "I tell him, 'William, you don't know how heavy your hand is.'"

"All it takes is one swat of that big hand, and he can knock you down," said Clemson assistant strength coach Don Telle.

But Latavia has survived. And her childlike innocence has served to

The Perrys—William, Sherry and daughter Latavia—are at home in Aiken in the summer of 1984.

keep things in proper perspective. During the shooting of the McDonald's commercial two days after the 44-0 victory over the Cowboys, Latavia arrived on the set in her daddy's arms. But when the cameras started rolling, Perry had to leave his daughter on the sideline. So impressed was Latavia with her father, the television star, she promptly fell asleep.

Everybody else had long since awoken to Perry's potential. The future was now. A hot team had caught a hot phenomenon and both were riding the other by the tail. Sure, the Bears might lose a few games. And sure, Perry might get injured, although that was unlikely. He had never missed a game in his life.

But the most interesting part of it all was pondering what might happen next to the Refrigerator and the Monsters of the Midway.

RECORD SECTION

MISCELLANEOUS INDIVIDUAL BEAR MARKS
(through the 1984 season)

SERVICE
Seasons, Active Player
14 Bill George, 1952-65
14 Doug Buffone, 1966-79
Games, Lifetime
186 Doug Buffone, 1966-79
186 Bob Parsons, 1972-83
Consecutive Games Lifetime
167 Bob Parsons, 1972-83
Seasons, Head Coach
40 George Halas, 1920-29, 1933-42,
1946-55, 1958-67

SCORING
Points, Lifetime
629 Bob Thomas, 1975-84 (245 xp,
128 fg)
Points, Season
132 Gale Sayers, 1965 (22 td)
Points, Game
36 Gale Sayers, 12/12/65

Touchdowns
Touchdowns, Lifetime
98 Walter Payton, 1975-84 (89 rush,
9 rec)
Touchdowns, Season
22 Gale Sayers, 1965 (14 rush, 6 rec,
2 ret)
Touchdowns, Game
6 Gale Sayers, 12/12/65 (4 rush, 1 rec,
1 ret)

Extra Points
Extra Points, Lifetime
247 George Blanda, 1949-58
Extra Points, Season
52 Roger Leclerc, 1965
Extra Points, Game
8 Bob Snyder, 11/14/43
Consecutive Extra Points, Lifetime
156 George Blanda, 10/28/51-10/21/56
Extra Points (no misses), Season
52 Roger Leclerc, 1965
Extra Points, (no misses), Game
8 Bob Snyder, 11/14/43

Field Goals
Field Goals, Lifetime
128 Bob Thomas, 1975-84
Field Goals, Season
25 Mac Percival, 1968
Field Goals, Game
5 Roger Leclerc, 12/3/61
5 Mac Percival, 10/20/68
Consecutive Field Goals, Lifetime
11 Bob Thomas, 11/11/84
Longest Field Goal
55 Bob Thomas, 11/23/75

RUSHING
Yardage
Yards Gained, Lifetime
13,309 Walter Payton, 1975-84
Yards Gained, Season
1,852 Walter Payton, 1977
Yards Gained, Game
275 Walter Payton, 11/20/77
Longest Run from Scrimmage
86 Bill Osmanski, (TD) 10/15/39

Touchdowns
Touchdowns, Lifetime
89 Walter Payton, 1975-84
Touchdowns, Season
14 Gale Sayers, 1965
14 Walter Payton, 1977
14 Walter Payton, 1979
Touchdowns, Game
4 Rick Casares, 10/28/56
4 Rick Casares, 12/6/59
4 Gale Sayers, 12/12/65
4 Bobby Douglass, 11/4/73

PASSING
Rating, Lifetime (400+passes)
82.0 Jim McMahon, 1982-84
Rating, Season (100+)
107.8 Sid Luckman, 1943

Completions
Completions, Lifetime
904 Sid Luckman, 1939-50
Completions, Season
225 Bill Wade, 1962
Completions, Game
33 Bill Wade, 10/25/64

Completion Percentage
*Completion Percentage, Lifetime
(250+comp.)*
58.6 Jim McMahon, 1982-84, 380 of 648
*Completion Percentage,
Season (60+)*
61.9 Rudy Bukich, 1964, 99 of 160
Completion Percentage, Game (10+)
86.7 Bob Williams, 10/12/52, 13 of 15

Yards Passing
Yards Passing, Lifetime
14,686 Sid Luckman, 1939-50
Yards Passing, Season
3,172 Bill Wade, 1962
Yards Passing, Game
468 Johnny Lujack, 12/11/49
Longest Pass Completion
98 Bill Wade (to John Farrington),
(TD) 10/8/61

Touchdown Passes
Touchdown Passes, Lifetime
137 Sid Luckman, 1939-50
Touchdown Passes, Season
28 Sid Luckman, 1943
Touchdown Passes, Game
7 Sid Luckman, 11/14/43

PASS RECEIVING
Pass Receptions, Lifetime
373 Walter Payton, 1975-84
Pass Receptions, Season
93 Johnny Morris, 1964
Pass Receptions, Game
14 Jim Keane, 10/23/49

Yards Gained
Yards Gained, Lifetime
5,059 Johnny Morris, 1958-67
Yards Gained, Season
1,200 Johnny Morris, 1964
Yards Gained, Game
214 Harlon Hill, 10/31/54
Longest Pass Reception
98 John Farrington (from Bill Wade),
(TD) 10/8/61

Touchdowns
Touchdowns, Lifetime
50 Ken Kavanaugh, 1940-41, 1945-50
Touchdowns, Season
13 Ken Kavanaugh, 1947
13 Dick Gordon, 1970
Touchdowns, Game
4 Harlon Hill, 10/31/54
4 Mike Ditka, 10/13/63

INTERCEPTIONS BY
Interceptions By, Lifetime
37 Richie Petitbon, 1959-68
Interceptions By, Season
9 Roosevelt Taylor, 1963
Interceptions By, Game
3 Hank Margarita, 11/11/45
3 Johnny Lujack, 9/26/48
3 Richie Petitbon, 9/24/67
3 Curtiss Gentry, 11/19/67
3 Ross Brupbacher, 12/12/76

Longest Interception Return
101 Richie Petitbon, (TD) 12/9/62

BEARS' NFL CHAMPIONSHIPS
1932—Chicago 9,
        Portsmouth (O.) Spartans 0
1933—Chicago 23, N.Y. Giants 21
1940—Chicago 73, Washington 0
1941—Chicago 37, N.Y. Giants 9
1943—Chicago 41, Washington 21
1946—Chicago 24, N.Y. Giants 14
1963—Chicago 14, N.Y. Giants 10

WILLIAM PERRY'S CLEMSON STATS

Year/School	Tackles/ Solos	Fumble Rec	Forced Fumble	Sacks/ Yards	TL/ Yds	Games/ Starts
1981 Clemson	48/33	2	1	4/44	9/50	12/4
1982 Clemson	52/30	1	3	5/38	9/66	11/7
1983 Clemson	61/38	1	2	6/40	15/67	11/4
1984 Clemson	100/69	3	2	10/68	27/111	11/11
TOTALS	261/170	7	8	25/190	60/294	45/26

64

Source: Chicago Bears 1985 Media Guide